I'M
BLACK

I'M
BLACK

EDITED BY

RUDY RASMUS

I'M
BLACK

I'm Christian.   I'm Methodist.

 Abingdon Press™

Nashville

I'M BLACK. I'M CHRISTIAN. I'M METHODIST.

Copyright © 2020 by Abingdon Press

ISBN: 9781791017095

Library of Congress Control Number: 2020947701

20 21 22 23 24 25 26 27 28 29—10 9 8 7 6 5 4 3 2 1
MANUFACTURED IN THE UNITED STATES OF AMERICA

CONTENTS

FOREWORD

Gregory Palmer

Resident Bishop, West Ohio

Annual Conference

In 1971 Marvin Gaye's *What's Going On* was released by Tamla Records. It was and is to this day a towering piece of social commentary. Every song on the album is about a world of chaos and an uneven social playing field. Gaye's riffs are global in scope, but there is an unmistakable emphasis on the tragic racialized history of America. The song "Inner City Blues" carries the subtitle "Make Me Wanna Holler." As I read through the essays in *I'm Black. I'm Christian. I'm Methodist,* I heard the lament of Marvin Gaye:

> Oh, make you wanna holler
>   the way they do my life.
> Make me wanna holler
>   the way they do my life.
> Oh, make me wanna holler
>   and throw up both my hands.
> Yeah, it makes me wanna holler
>   and throw up both my hands.

These lyrics from the early 1970s carry with them the mournful cry of the African American Spiritual tradition, such as "Nobody Knows the Trouble I've Seen." The confluence of the everyday indignities of being Black in America; the outrageous, egregious, legalized lynching of George Floyd; and the unforgivable disparities exposed once again by COVID–19 have conspired together to create a seminal moment in America and in The United Methodist Church—in which we must find the courage to say unambiguously *Black Lives Matter. Black Life Matters.* To stumble or choke on those words is beneath the gospel. To play them off against a litany of what I call "matter phrases" is avoidance. To dismiss the phrase and its truth because it has intentionally, unfairly, and disingenuously been painted with a brush whose only purpose is to smear it and hope it will go away is a colossal failure of nerve.

These essays weave together autobiography and spiritual formation. They represent, individually and collectively, a huge contribution to the genre of biography as theology. As well the writers confront each and all of us with the pain of their societal and institutional experiences when it comes to race. The intersectionality of the "isms" that bedevil the human family, America, and the Methodist tradition are not left in the margins but moved to a prominent place on the stage. Every writer in her or his own way says: *see me, hear me, deal with me, because—no matter what—I am not going away even if my institutional affiliation changes.* And that should not be expected.

"What then shall we say to all these things?" I hope as you read these narratives of hurt and hope you will think and pray deeply about our future together in the world, in America, and in the church. Reading *I'm Black. I'm Christian. I'm Methodist* is not intended to be an exercise in feeling only. While it is not in the technical sense a manifesto, it is a clarion call to "do justice, embrace faithful love, and walk humbly" (Mic 6:8). I began with a song and I close with another, the refrain from Harold Melvin and The Blue Notes, in their timeless "Wake Up Everybody":

The world won't get no better if we just let it be.
The world won't get no better; we gotta change it yeah, just you and me.

I'M (REALLY) BLACK.
I'M (AMAZINGLY) CHRISTIAN.
I'M METHODIST (FOR NOW).

Rudy Rasmus

Senior Pastor, St. Johns United Methodist Church, Houston, Texas

I'm (Really) Black.

My life journey began in Houston, Texas, on June 9, 1956, in the colored section of Hermann Hospital. My only documented proof of that moment came in the form of a hospital memento stamped with the inked bottoms of my tiny feet on day one of life. I held on to that certificate of birth for years as confirmation that I was actually somebody special. I'm the only child of Rudolph Valentino Rasmus, a Black college-educated hustler, and Mildred Thomas Rasmus, a farm girl raised on the former plantation of her White great-grandparents in the central Texas town of Caldwell, which was inherited by her biracial grandmother and still farmed today by her brothers. My mother and father were from two separate worlds. My mother's family owned land and cattle, and were a fiercely independent people. They were the enslaved decendents of Major Hugo Oldham, a wealthy White

1

plantation owner with two families: a White wife and children and a Black wife and children. When Major Oldham died, his last will and testament named his Black decendents as heirs. A court battle immediately followed when Major Oldham's White family petitioned the court to remove his Black family from the land, but, amazingly, Major Oldham's Black wife and her children prevailed in court, and a large portion of the estate was conveyed to his Black decendents. My mother is one of those decendents.

A few years ago, I decided to send a saliva sample to a genetic engineering company that provided extensive personal information based on one's DNA findings. When I received the email containing the results, I quickly opened it to find that I was a unique amalgamation of people groups spanning the entire globe. The following results piqued my interest: sub-Saharan–West African—67.8%; European—26.9%; East Asian—4.8%; and Middle Eastern—0.5%. The unequivocal results: I'm Black, and there was some obvious abuse placed on my ancestors.

As a child, I saw that the path to success was paved by loyalty, friendship, connections, and, in my family, the suspicion of religion. Observing my dad and his friends taught me about the power of relationships and how the different levels of privilege based on race, class, and gender could work for you and against you simultaneously. Also, it was from watching Dad and his friends that I learned that visualization and encouragement were two essentials of success, and that success in large part was connected to shared visions and a collective will. It was in my childhood that I realized that if you couldn't see it, you could, with the right synergy, achieve it, so from an early age I began to visualize a better outcome in the midst of dark, cloudy childhood moments, and religious experiences were not a part of my reality.

My father's older sister raised him from the time he was twelve years old. I called her Auntie MaeMae, and she was my connection to everything religious. It was the constant abuse she experienced at the hands of a violent, maniacal husband, and her repeated willingness to forgive him as an activity endorsed by Jesus himself, that left me thinking Christianity was too weak to respond to the real challenges facing my everyday life. It was one of many encounters with power that left me questioning the validity of religion and curious about the church's inability to access power as an institution responsible for the liberation of oppressed people, and especially Black people in America. I felt this as a child primarily because of the powerlessness of the church in changing the conditions in my world as an eight-year-old. I grew up in Houston, Texas, which had two doors: a front door for White people and a back door for Blacks, and I never liked it. I grew up in a world with a seating chart on public transportation, and it was understood that I was going to sit in the back because I was Black, and I never liked sitting on the back of anything, especially a bus. I also grew up in a world with two water fountains: one fountain was marked "Whites Only," and the other fountain was marked "Coloreds Only." I was always baffled by the existence of these two fountains, knowing in my mind and heart that only one fountain was needed. My curious mind would ask the question, "What is so different about that water?" As fearful as my mother would get when I got too close to that fountain reserved for "Whites Only," I knew there was something powerful about that water, and I imagined the church was too important to effect any substantive change in that arrangement. As a result of never feeling connected to the religious experience of my childhood church, I walked away from the church when I was twelve years old with no expectations of ever returning.

My return to church happened as a by-product of being recruited by the person who became my wife, Juanita. It worked. I returned, and after attending church for five years until one day after spending an intense year of weekly conversations with Willie Lane, I became a part of the religious establishment. Twenty-eight years ago, Juanita and I planted a church in downtown Houston with the help of my friend and mentor, Kirbyjon Caldwell. It was in a dilapidated building surrounded by homeless, crack-addicted people. Early in our experience as pastors, I began to realize how polarized the church was along the lines of race, class, gender, and sexual orientation. It was in this setting that I was introduced to the power of love, forgiveness, and authenticity. It was also in this context that I realized the net impact of the church's shift from the cultural center of society to the periphery of society—and the departure of young Black Americans from the ranks of church attenders was signaling the end of a church era.

Many reasons caused the church to become irrelevant to younger Black Americans, but the disorientating dilemma facing the Western church lies in its inability to reconcile a reasonable response to what Victor Anderson deemed "ontological Blackness." The church's waning cultural relevance continues to erode its credibility as a safe place for religious practice. In light of this erosion, I think the Black American religious experience is headed toward a schismatic collision with traditional Western religion. Syncretistic religious expressions expand as a result of the failure of current Western Christianity to present a postcolonial religious option that could undergird the realities of daily life in a polarized world.

In spite of the generational schism occurring in our world, I feel a sense of solidarity with my younger counterparts. I call them "Generation Why" throughout this chapter as a take on the prevailing question of this demographic group, "Why does church matter?" Historical expressions of the Black church undergirded the harshness and cruelty of life with hopeful imagination. Now we are in the midst of a Black global uprising of epic proportions as our nation and the world grapple with its racist past and present-day transgressions. "Why does church matter?" is also the question facing the religious complex as the world faces a global pandemic caused by COVID-19 and the accompanying economic collapse.

My life has been replete with many surprising turns, and I'm a product of each of those turns, complete with all of the thrills, traumas, tests, and triumphs. This journey created immense daily tension for me as a Black person struggling to see my place in a world that channels contempt for me. I often ask, "What have I done to deserve this other than being born Black?" As I continue the search for meaning as a Christian and a Methodist, I fully understand why young Black Americans are either walking away from the religious experience of their Christian forebears or never attempting to cross the threshold of a church into that experience. So each contributor in this book asks, "Can Black people justify being Christian, and does Methodism offer future hope?"

I'm (Amazingly) Christian.

My father taught me never to trust preachers and church people. He would say they are only after the money. The lack of trust in the religious establishment gelled in Black American culture between the 1930s and 1950s. The distrust solidified in the1960s during the first revolution. This lack of trust has an iron grip on today's generation. I believe the great undoing of the church's prominence in society began when church leaders started focusing on numerical and financial growth as the benchmarks of success, while ignoring the fact that government policies were put in place that would ultimately incarcerate millions of Black people who had become victims of state-sponsored drug addiction. Millions of missing Black people who could have potentially become participants of organized religion vanished to prisons and into the dark crevices of drug culture while the ideological turn from the church as a proponent for civil justice became a mission to build mega-ministries with prosperous participants. The unfortunate part of the American success story is the Western Christian church's participation in how it provided religious sanctions to culture's ravenous excess and insatiable greed, as it mimicked the materially self-indulgent Western culture's penchant for prosperity. This addiction to material prosperity was a contingent benefit of at least four hundred years of free slave labor, which spawned religious, economic, and political doctrines that supported and undergirded the atrocity of slavery for centuries and even until today.

Dad was tricked by a professional con man when he was in his early twenties, and he was hypervigilant for the next fifty years by looking for a con until he died in 2004. The trick was called the "pigeon drop" because the trickster would attract the prospective victim's attention by dropping a dead pigeon in front of the person and wait for a compassionate reaction. The dialogue would always encompass the victim, assumed to be the recipient of a benefit without doing anything for the benefit while making a financial investment with the professional huckster to show the victim's commitment to the scheme. My dad always viewed the pastor and the related request for financial offerings as a form of the old "pigeon drop," and he resisted subsequently to give validity to religion. Amazingly, Dad joined St. John's and converted to Christianity in our seventh year of ministry and became one of our top givers. When asked one day about his change of heart in relation to church membership, he replied, "I finally found a pastor I could trust." The running joke around our family for years was the fact that he was referring to Juanita and not me (his son).

The unfortunate side effect of the American success story is the church's participation in how it gave a platform to insatiably greedy con men and con women, as it mimicked the materially self-indulgent American culture. Bruce Birch and Larry Rasmussen declared, "When a church does what it is supposed to do, as a church, it transforms not only the lives of its members but the life of their culture as well."[1] Well, the church has failed. Kate Bowler, in her book *Blessed: A History of the American Prosperity Gospel*, chronicles the Black sojourn from oppressive Jim Crow South to Northern cities in the 1920s and 1930s, where those who had been exposed to more traditional expressions of religious doctrine began to encounter spiritualism, New Thought, hypnosis, mesmerism, and other metaphysical expressions of religion. Religious leaders like Reverend Ike and Daddy Grace "promised to smooth the rough edges of capitalism and industrialism with theologies that countered poverty, disease, and despair."[2] Black theological modifiers took the original product of Essek William Kenyon, considered the grandfather of the modern faith-message

1. Bruce Birch and Larry Rasmussen, *The Bible and Ethics in the Christian Life* (Minneapolis: Augsburg Fortress, 1988).
2. Kate Bowler, *Blessed: A History of the American Prosperity Gospel* (New York: Oxford University Press, 2018), 25.

movement, offered religious solutions to economic woes, and made it culturally relevant to masses of Blacks who were leaving the Jim Crow South for a better quality of life in the industrializing Northern American cities. The message of physical health, financial wealth, and good fortune as divine repayment for doctrinal and ritual compliance attracted millions of impoverished Black and White Americans, the number of which ultimately exploded along with the prosperity church movement, and which gradually waned as younger culture changed its opinion on the ethics of religious prosperity. The prosperity gospel at its peak represented American triumphalism as religious pseudo-entertainers mastered the fusion of Black Pentecostalism, New Thought, and metaphysical religion. The syncretism opened an escape hatch for its devotees from the oppressive regimen of poverty, which held communities of color hostage for centuries in America. The escape was created by a distinctive thread of prosperity theology within Black religious culture, which became the fuel of Black megachurches nationwide as church attendance exploded along with new economies and optimism.

The tension for me in ministry has always involved balancing my gangster proclivities with my love for Jesus and people. My early years in ministry at St. John's United Methodist Church were preoccupied with driving membership growth. The formula was magical for the first twenty years, and we were successful because our first surge of church attenders in the early 1990s were part of the generation of baby boomers (born between 1946–1964) who were materially focused and success-driven following the end of the war in Vietnam. In many ways, the church became a social outlet for adults, a youth entertainment venue, and a facility-focused mammoth that took very seriously serving the needs of our homeless and hungry neighbors. One thing on my mind constantly was the absolute requirement to not fulfill my father's diminished view of pastoral integrity by making a misstep that could call into question the validity of Christianity.

As a Buddhist in college and during an interest in Islam during my post-college years, I was fascinated with the fact that Black people were, in large part, Christian in America in spite of the atrocities of the slave trade and the transgressions of the church, the cosigner for the slave industry. I asked my wife one morning, "How did the descendants of African slaves become Christians in the midst of the intentional misinterpretation of biblical scriptures and the dissipation of anything resembling the character of love represented throughout those scriptures?" Her answer was swift and concise. She said, "It was somehow through divine dispensation the descendants encountered the spirit of the slave-holder's religion and not the malicious interpretations of their intent." Cornel West speaks with poignant clarity to zealous Christian traditions when he suggests it "began the moment that slaves, laboring in sweltering heat on the plantations owned and ruled primarily by White American Christians, tried to understand their lives and servitude in light of biblical texts, Protestant hymns, and Christian testimonies."[3] He puts into perspective the "miracle," revealed in the decisions of slaves to create a religious rubric, "This miracle came into being when slaves decided, often at the risk of life and limb, to make Jesus their choice and to share with one another their common Christian sense of purpose and

---

3. Cornel West, *Prophesy Deliverance* (Louisville, KY: Westminster John Knox, 2002), 15.

Christian understanding of their circumstances insisting upon both otherworldly salvation as the proper loci of Christianity."[4]

Among the many American generations moving through history's timeline are 70 million people between eighteen and forty years old filled with palpable suspicion of the church's intent. This distrust is valid, and one way to transcend this cynicism is by presenting a balanced and honest narrative of the Christian faith. Just as the slaves brought their life experiences to bear on early Black Christianity, we too, in the age of global pandemics and the dire impact of climate change, must look for ways to more powerfully connect our current life circumstances with our faith, rather than resting on our traditional models of gathering, which are nearly extinct. Disruption in the Christian church has already taken place (1) as it grapples to understand church on computer screens and imposed by in-person limits, and (2) as we get truthful about the obvious decline in participation that started long before the COVID-19 pandemic.

Today, I'm amazingly Christian in spite of how White supremacist heteropatriarchy and racial capitalism used the faith for dominance and power. I'm amazingly Christian in spite of the silence of my non-Black peers in ministry across all denominational lines. Finally, I'm Christian because I believe a combination of love and resistance can make a difference in the presence of a landscape lacking moral leadership and possessing a weakened political will in the face of a historic global pandemic, a crippling economic recession, and growing social unrest at the outbreak of police violence enacted against Black Americans.

---

4. West, *Prophesy Deliverance*, 15.

I'm Methodist (For Now)

I became Methodist by accident. My encounter was accidental because I was not a Christian or a church attendee when I walked through the doors at Windsor Village United Methodist Church in 1985 shortly after marrying Juanita and at the invitation of an old friend. Attending church was part of our agreement as newlyweds, so I walked in as a suspicious agnostic on my first Sunday. To my surprise, I heard the familiar presence of liberation talk from the pulpit. I was shocked, impressed, and I had an inner feeling that the church we were attending was uniquely suited for me.

"Why am I Methodist?" The answer is complicated. First, I'm Methodist because I was invited to a relevant church experience and liked it enough to stay, but honestly, few churches would have presented a compelling enough reason for me to stay long enough to see myself as a possible devotee of the faith. Pastor Caldwell was a compelling leader and introduced himself to me on my second visit to the church. We became friends almost immediately, and much to my surprise, he didn't shrink away when he discovered I owned and operated a borderline bordello at the time. It was the power of acceptance that opened the door to quieting my skepticism. The fact that Windsor Village was a United Methodist church meant nothing to me at the time, but the presence of a Black theological perspective coupled with economic self-reliance registered deeply. I sat on the pew of that church for five years as a nonbeliever, but became entangled by the love I received as an attendee. In my fifth year of attending services, I converted to Christianity, and two years later became the pastor of a Methodist congregation in downtown Houston. Over the past twenty-eight

11

years, I have questioned my affiliation with the United Methodist Church on multiple occasions. In 2020, I'm questioning my affiliation more often than ever as the global denomination approaches a probable schism based on differing views regarding the inclusion of LGBTQIA Christians. With my view based on full inclusion of all people regardless of sexual identity, I'm in solidarity with about half the denomination's leaders who feel patriarchy, sexism, and homophobia will distance the church even further from cultural relevancy or transformation, and will ultimately eliminate unifying possibilities for the future.

John Wesley's movement in its day caused institutional disruption to the hierarchical systems that governed the Church of England. In the same way the COVID-19 pandemic has disrupted the American church. The whole world has radically changed in ways yet to be seen, and so have the socioeconomic mechanisms the Black church has depended on for decades, forcing institutions of color to face their relevance to society and sustainability in a demonetized environment. No longer will sermons and songs be the sole determining factor on the significance of any particular house of worship. If the church is expected to be the cultural expression of Christianity for Black society in the future, with the ultimate goal of encouraging a new generation of practitioners to make Jesus their choice, the church will be faced with distinct challenges.

There is a void in the religious ecosphere for gatherings of engaging, productive, intellectual, and innovative churches in mission with "Black Generation Why." Black Methodist churches have a unique opportunity to bridge that void. A contextual critique of my current setting is prioritizing the curation of innovative methodologies for gathering Generation Why, in part by utilizing collaborative inquiry as a pedagogy for fostering new faith communities. There are three ideas the Black church should consider implementing to shift the downward spiral of departure from Black Methodist churches:

1. Create culturally relevant nonreligious themes designed to attract younger Black adults, with the goal of creating relationships, introducing Christianity, and deepening personal spirituality. Relevant themes require an environment that honors and acknowledges sociocultural differences while being sensitive to the learning context that makes room for forming belief, so that Black culture is saturated in the learning context, all the while leaving room for the healthy suspicion that the traditional Black church can go astray with the prosperity gospel or the pursuit of mega-ministry.

2. Develop an all-inclusive learning context, which integrates feeling with cognitive knowing, and by expanding awareness about the effects in Black neighborhoods of White supremacy and anti-Black racism. The learning needs to address the origins of racism, the chronological history of racism, and the racial discrimination that is the genesis of every racist action. An authentic, transparent pedagogy will intuitively create an environment safe for the level of reflection needed to counter negative assumptions about personal faith while revealing the benefit to the community as a whole.

3. Provide safe places for critical reflection on commonly held assumptions. By listening and creating dialogue in smaller affinity groups, which necessitates a shift in focus from numerical growth to effective cohesion, the church should be a place to explore the immeasurable negative

effects from the implications of postcolonial religious ideologies. The net impact of the church's shift from the cultural center to the periphery of society has been felt in the departure of younger Americans and specifically young Black Americans.

Finally, I'm Methodist because I believe the polity of The United Methodist Church (unlike many denominations) provides a potential framework for the exploration of the immeasurable negative effects of postcolonial religious ideologies on Black people. Scholars like Eddie Glaude believe "too often the prophetic energies of Black churches are represented as something inherent to the institution, and we need only point to past deeds for evidence of this fact."[5] The Black church will not be able to point to past deeds or decades as the source of credibility in these crucial times. The brutal murder of George Floyd has emblazoned an image on the hearts and minds of Black people as the world watched in horror and disbelief when his life was taken one breath at a time through the symbol of oppression: a knee on his neck. The words "I can't breathe" become a symbol of a people who have been suffocating for four centuries while waiting for Jesus to do something about their predicament. The Uprising of 2020 is the moment, the opportunity for the church to redeem its place in the movement toward countering racial injustice with new warriors cut from the religious cloth of the next generation, asking Why? We must make room for new theological minds, openness to new experiences, and a willingness to revisit the focus and meaning of prophetic witness with the absolute goal of

5. Eddie Glaude Jr., "The Black Church Is Dead," March 26, 2010, *HuffPost*, http://www.huffingtonpost.com/eddie-glaude-jr-phd/the Black-church-is-dead-_b _473815.html.

increasing relevancy and participation. No longer can we point to the way we were. The future is only as bright as the church is willing to break out the stained glass windows that have for centuries blocked out a view of the outside world—and to look deeply into the eyes of the people who walk away as a result of the church's myopic view. Black lives matter, Black churches matter, and so do the Black Christians who inhabit them.

We're Black.
We're Christians.
We're Methodists.

It's uncertain that Howard Thurman made the remark often attributed to him, "I have been writing this book all my life," but there is little doubt that he was deeply immersed in reflection on the times that bear an uncanny resemblance to the present day. Our "life's book" is filled with sentence upon sentence of marginalization, pages of apartheid, chapters of separate and unequal. Now this season reveals volumes of violence against Blacks in America. In the following chapters, my colleagues explore life through the lens of their own religious narratives. They are people whose lives are tangible demonstrations of the power of a divine purpose, and evidence of what grace really means in the face of hardship, disappointment, and determination. Each of our journeys intersect, because of three central elements that are the focus of this book. We're Black. We're Christians. We're Methodists. And for the record, we're also friends.

Chapter Two

I'M BLACK. I'M YOUNG. I'M A WOMAN. AND I'M GRIEVED.

Tori C. Butler

Lead Pastor, Good Hope Union United Methodist Church,
Silver Spring, Maryland

I'm Black. I'm young. I'm a woman. I'm Methodist. And I'm grieved. Every time I go to my office a symbol of my grief rests on my desk, looking back at me. It's a stained-glass cross given to me as a graduation gift from my seminary. This cross represents the racial discrimination that became apparent as I sat in classes where I was the only Black student. This cross represents the immense financial burden I received because of pursuing higher education in order to be affirmed as a United Methodist pastor. This cross represents the stained glass brick ceiling that existed for me because I dared to be young, gifted, Black, and a woman. The cross represents the hope that, despite the hardships I've faced, I still serve a God who says, "I am the resurrection and the life" (John 11:25). I grieve because I have hope that God will restore my dreams for my life, my ministry, for the ministries of other Black clergywomen, and for what The United Methodist Church can be.

Grief and the Burden of the StrongBlackWoman

According to psychiatrist Collin Murray Parkes, grief is "an emotion that draws us toward something or someone that is missing. It arises from the awareness of a discrepancy between the world that is and the world that 'should be.'"[6] The desire to live into the world that "should be" pushes many of us to fight and resist loss; but loss is a part of life. Elisabeth Kübler-Ross and David Kessler argue that "we cannot grow without loss."[7] Therefore, grief is unavoidable. It has the ability to teach us something about ourselves and the social locations in which we reside. We do ourselves a disservice when we try to mask or hide the emotions that often accompany grief. And yet, as a young Black female who was trained in a Methodist seminary and would go on to serve as clergy, I wasn't always free to express my grief. I was afraid to express discontent out of fear that I would upset the wrong person and impede my ordination process or hinder my opportunity to serve in a "good appointment." Therefore, I had become so accustomed to suffering in private that I just accepted it as a way of life. I unconsciously embraced the trope of the StrongBlackWoman. Chanequa Walker-Barnes describes the StrongBlackWoman as

> a modern day Atlas, she bears the weight of her multiple worlds upon her shoulders. And unfortunately, she is as incapable of saying "help" as she is of saying "no." . . . Thus, fearful of being seen as unfaithful, the StrongBlackWoman invests considerable effort in

6. Collin Murray Parkes, "Bereavement as a Psychological Transition: Processes of Adaptation to Change," in *Handbook of Bereavement: Theory, Research, and Intervention* (New York: Cambridge University Press, 1993), 92.

7. Elisabeth Kübler-Ross, MD, and David Kessler, *Life Lessons: Two Experts on Death and Dying Teach Us About the Mysteries of Life and Living* (New York: Scribner, 2000), 78.

maintaining the appearance of strength and suppresses all behaviors, emotions, and thoughts that might contradict or threaten that image. Even as the physical and psychological toll of her excessive caregiving mount up, she maintains a façade of having it all together and being in control.[8]

Where did this burden come from and why did I feel the need to live into this identity of StrongBlackWoman, to my detriment?

History of Becoming a Commodity

African American women are descendants of slaves who survived the cruelty of the transatlantic slave trade, the savagery of slavery, and then were terrorized, disenfranchised, and dehumanized by the Jim Crow South. Kelly Brown Douglas observes that during slavery Black bodies were considered chattel—"to be chattel mean[t] that Black people did not have the right to possess their bodies. They did not own them. Neither did they have the right to possess other Black bodies, not even those of their children. In this regard, the chatteled Black body is not cherished property. It is instead a valued commodity."[9] In other words, the bodies of Black men and women only had value contingent upon how much they could produce. In 1776,

> when the authors of the Declaration of Independence proclaimed
> that all men were created equal and endowed with unalienable
> rights, that meant "men" literally and White men specifically.[10]

8. Chanequa Walker-Barnes, *Too Heavy a Yoke: Black Women and the Burden of Strength* (Eugene, OR: Cascade Books, 2014), 4–5.

9. Kelly Brown Douglas, *Stand Your Ground: Black Bodies and the Justice of God* (Maryknoll, NY: Orbis Books, 2015), 53.

10. Paula S. Rothenberg, *Race, Class, and Gender in the United States: An Integrated Study*, 6th ed. (New York,: Worth Publishers, 2004), 437.

Article 1, Section 2 of the United States Constitution contains a clause called the three-fifths compromise that deems enslaved Negroes (the term used to describe Black people at the time) to be counted as three-fifths of a person for the sake of determining taxes and representation of the states in Congress.[11] The worth of Black people was limited to their labor and not in their human dignity. They were forced to learn dehumanizing survival skills to avoid persecution, abuse, rape, and death.

Before and long after the Civil War, Black people struggled to have their personhood recognized. They lived in the tension of having to be accepted in both Black and White social circles. W. E. B. DuBois calls this experience double-consciousness, which

> is a peculiar sensation . . . this sense of always looking at one's self through the eyes of others, of measuring one's soul by the tape of a world that looks on in amused contempt and pity. One ever feels his twoness,—an American, a Negro; two souls, two thoughts, two reconciled strivings; two warring ideals in one dark body, whose dogged strength alone keeps it from being torn asunder.[12]

Being Black in America is its own yoke, but being Black and female is an additional set of issues; for instance, being labeled as angry or aggressive when not afraid to voice one's opinions, receiving lower pay for equal or better work than White or male counterparts. Teresa Fry Brown addresses this tension in her book *Can a Sistah Get a Little Help?: Encouragement for Black Women in Ministry* when she says,

> Though African women were mothers, priests, and queen mothers who served as keepers of the traditions and rituals, a stark feature

---

11.　Rothenberg, *Race, Class, and Gender in the United States*, 437.

12.　W. E. B. DuBois, *The Souls of Black Folk* (Brooklyn, NY: Restless Books, 2017), 9.

of African American women's existence has been their invisibility, isolation, tokenism, and exclusion from societal privilege.[13]

Historically, when Black women were rejected by the world, they found solace in the church. They were able to establish an identity as pastor, evangelist, church mother, deaconess, missionary, pastor's wife, teacher—whatever the community needed them to be. Through their position they could expect or even demand respect. But even in the Black church, the institution where "Black leadership, culture, traditions, experience, and spirituality represent the norm, and from which White Anglo-Saxon traditions and expressions are fairly absent,"[14] Black women are still seen as less than and often have to bulldoze their way or use a sledgehammer to break through what Brown calls the "brick ceiling."[15]

In my youth, I had the unique opportunity to observe the leadership of four Black clergywomen serving as senior pastor of my home United Methodist church in Baltimore. All the women were anointed and gifted, but I watched them have to fight for respect from the congregation. I watched other Black women in the church challenge their leadership. I watched as the church held high expectations for the fruitfulness of their ministries while offering little certainty about their salaries. I watched them be faithful even when they were assigned two- or three-point charges of churches that were dying, and buildings that were falling to pieces. I watched them beat at the brick ceiling and never get through. These women showed me how to be a StrongBlack-

13.   Teresa L. Fry Brown, *Can a Sistah Get a Little Help?: Encouragement for Black Women in Ministry* (Cleveland: Pilgrim Press, 2008), xii.

14.   Anthony G. Reddie, *Black Theology in Transatlantic Dialogue* (New York: Palgrave McMillan, 2007), 48.

15.   Fry Brown, *Can a Sistah Get a Little Help?* xxvii.

Woman; but they also showed me how to persevere and depend on God despite the dire circumstances of the church.

The Impact of the Stained Glass, Brick Ceiling

In the words of Langston Hughes, "Life for me ain't been no crystal stair."[16] Ever since I was a child, I attempted to break the stained glass, brick ceiling over my head. I call it stained glass brick because it represents the multilayered oppression that I've experienced because I'm young, Black, a woman, and an ordained United Methodist clergywoman. The first awareness of this stained glass brick ceiling appeared in seminary. I went to seminary because I heard the Lord say, "Life is too short not to serve me." I truly believed that God set a fire within me, and I wanted to do everything I could do to be connected to God. I had hoped that seminary would disciple me. It didn't do that; but it did teach me how to think theologically. It also introduced me to a form of Methodism that I didn't know and didn't like. I grew up in Baltimore, which is a predominantly Black city. My home church was located in a low-income area. And, I didn't grow up in a super churchy household. Thus, the Whitewashed form of Methodism I was taught in graduate school was foreign to me. It was challenging to sit in Methodist classes that consisted of twelve, thirty-five, or seventy-five students and be the only Black person in the class. I remember only one class in the entire curriculum devoted to teaching about Black Methodism. This grieved my whole being:

16. Langston Hughes, "Mother to Son," in *Selected Poems of Langston Hughes: A Classical Collection of Poems by a Master of Verse*, 6th ed. (New York: Vintage Books, 1990), 187.

how could I serve a church who doesn't value the contributions of people who look like me? After all, there is a John Wesley in my family: John Wesley Roberts who built Roberts Tabernacle CME (Colored now Christian Methodist Episcopal Church) in 1885. Black folk have been Methodists for a very long time. And yet it isn't the story that is told. I truly contemplated not being Methodist because of my experience in the classroom.

Then something changed. My final project in a course on twentieth-century Methodism was a mock version of commissioning papers (part of the ordination process for deacons and elders). In this paper, I had to research and understand three types of grace—prevenient grace, justifying grace, and sanctifying grace. Prevenient grace is God's all-encompassing love for you that is in action even before you recognize God. Justifying grace is God's saving grace. It is the moment or process of conversion; when your yes combines with God's yes. Sanctifying grace is the work of the Holy Spirit. It is when the Holy Spirit begins to cleanse you from the inside out and pushes you to look more like Christ daily. Learning these three types of grace changed everything for me. My heart became strangely warmed not just for Christ but for the opportunity to introduce others to the life transforming love of God. Suddenly I had hope in the possibilities of what The United Methodist Church could be. It could be a culture where the grace of God is offered to all, no matter their race, color, gender, ethnicity, or age. It could be a space where all have a seat at God's table and taste and see that God's love is available not just for some but for all.

The inclusive grace might sound idealistic to some, but I really believed in the possibilities of what The United Methodist Church could be. However, that stained glass brick ceiling was still blocking the vision. It made an appearance in my first appointment. I served in a cross-racial appointment in Southeast Texas. This part of Texas was known to be openly racist. A few miles away from where I served was a town that I was instructed as a Black person to never visit—if I wanted to come back home. Having this location so close to where I served should have been a major red flag; but all I could see was ministry. My church was located across the street from a funeral home, catty-corner from a local community college, three blocks from a housing project, located downtown, and had four kitchens but didn't have a feeding program. In my heart, mind, and spirit I felt like this church had major potential to do some amazing transformational ministry in the community. But, as much as my senior pastor said he prepared the congregation to receive me, I didn't realize that they were NOT READY AT ALL! I was the first Black staff person who didn't clean the floors. I was only the second woman to serve in a pastoral role at that church. I was young, Black, a woman, and from the East Coast. I had left behind my momma, the rest of my family, my friends, and the promise of a good-paying job to pursue ministry. Upon my arrival, there were roaches falling from the ceiling in my parsonage. There were fire ants in the driveway that ate up my legs. There were people who had never met a young Black woman who didn't clean their house or work as a home health care nurse. I had people either touch or attempt to touch my hair, and I would tell them that it was culturally inappropriate to do that. My authority would be challenged through a series of microaggressions that at times made my job challenging to accomplish. These microaggressions got amplified during a staff change of a long standing employee. I became a target, since the time after my arrival is when things started to change. I began to receive racist emails, and I no longer felt safe at the church. Therefore, after six months of serving there I was gone.

This experience shaped my ministry. I really took on the persona of the StrongBlackWoman. I offered grace to people who had no grace to offer me. I served communion to people who would never welcome me at their table. I learned how to love those who loved me but also those who harassed me. I discovered that I was a bridge between Black and White folk, as well as the affluent and the indigent. I worked tirelessly to be accepted within the White contexts that I served. I dealt with being isolated by location and at times nominally supported. I also had to learn how to navigate people who were determined to classify me as an "other." For instance, during the commissioning process clergy are subject to psychological evaluations. In that meeting, I was asked by the White evaluator, "Are you angry?" I had to take a deep breath because I thought to myself, *How many White people did he ask this question*? I felt like the question was asked to trigger an angry response. I calmly responded, "No, I'm not angry. I get frustrated sometimes." Although, on the inside I was boiling mad because here is the stained glass brick ceiling showing up not just in the local church I serve but also within the system.

I'm reminded of the invisible barrier of the stained glass brick ceiling every time someone tells me "you look like a little girl" because they can't imagine a young Black woman who accepted her call early in life as a senior pastor of a church. I'm reminded of the stained glass brick ceiling every time I think about making more money as an intern at a utility company in college than I did in my first two appointments. I'm reminded of the stained glass brick ceiling when I think of receiving the same training of some of my White male counterparts but not given the same opportunities. I'm reminded of the stained glass brick ceiling when I was asked to preach and everyone in the room was called "pastor" or "reverend," but because I was young and a woman, I was called "sister." I'm reminded of the stained glass brick ceiling when I think of the moments when I preached in non-Methodist settings and I was not allowed to sit or preach in the pulpit. I'm reminded of the stained glass brick ceiling when I remember looking around the room of young recruits for pastor under age thirty-five, and for years not one looked like me. I'm grieved by this stained glass brick ceiling that I have faced and other young, Black, women, clergy face in the United Methodist conferences.

Learning How to Holler

After serving in full-time ministry for ten years in The United Methodist Church, I realized I needed to do something with my grief. I could not allow the stained-glass brick ceiling to hold me hostage. I didn't want to continue living in a chained existence. I wanted to be free. So I began to think about the ways my ancestors "got over." I asked the question, "How did they grieve?" In other words, how did they acknowledge their loss while living in the tension of what is and what they hoped for? The answer is that they engaged in the ancient Jewish practice of lament. Lament is crying out to God and expecting God to respond. It's individual and communal. It's an understanding that we can tell God about our troubles, and God won't leave us there. All lament should end in praise. But, when lament is placed in the mouths of Black women, it becomes a holler. It is a cry coming from the depths of their bellies that names injustice and oppression but presses toward a hope that can only come from a redemptive God.

A. Elaine Brown Crawford illustrates in her book, *A Hope in the Holler: A Womanist Theology*, that the

> Holler is the primal cry of pain, abuse, violence, separation. It is a soul-piercing shrill of the African ancestors that demands the recognition and appreciation of their humanity. The Holler is the refusal to be silenced in a world that denied their very existence as women. The Holler is the renunciation of racialized and genderized violence perpetrated against them generation after generation. The Holler is a cry to God to "come see about me," one of your children.[17]

When we lament and holler, we are giving our grief a sound. We are giving voice to our pain so that freedom and release can occur.

Jephthah's daughter in Judges 11 is who really taught me how to holler. She is condemned to death because her father made a foolish vow to God that if God would give him victory in battle, he would sacrifice whatever came out of his house first. Unfortunately, it was his daughter. Jephthah blames her for his thoughtless commitment. Jephthah told her, "'Oh no, my daughter! You have brought me down and I am devastated. I have made a vow to the LORD that I cannot break'" (Judg 11:35b NIV). In the CEB, Jephthah said, "You have brought me to my knees!" The NRSV states that Jephthah proclaimed, "You have brought me very low." The NLT says that Jephthah declared "You have completely destroyed me! You've brought disaster on me!" At this moment, Jephthah's daughter hid her emotions and reacted calmly to the hysterics of her father. She responded, "My father, you've opened your mouth to the LORD, so you should do to me just what you've promised. After all, the LORD has carried out just punishment

---

17. A. Elaine Brown Crawford, *Hope In the Holler: A Womanist Theology* (Louisville, KY: Westminster John Knox Press, 2002), xii.

for you on your enemies the Ammonites" (Judg 11:36). But in the same breath this woman whose power was taken away, whose identity was tied to her father and to her father's rash promise, took away his power by choosing how she wanted to exit the earth. She didn't want to spend her last days with the one who victimized her. She requested that she and her girlfriends have two months to roam the hills and to weep. The scripture said she wept because she would never marry. In this moment, she wept for her future.

Jephthah's daughter designed her own memorial service. And in it she decided to surround herself with a community of women, women who were just like her, women who understood what true sorrow and grief looked like. Barbara Miller noticed,

> There is a sorrow known only to women; a sorrow so profound and so bottomless, it can only be shared with a woman; a sorrow that only another woman can help you bear. It comes from being violated, betrayed, and abandoned by a force much stronger than yourself. And when the force is someone you trusted, the sorrow can be unbearable.[18]

These women understood that the fate of Jephthah's daughter could be theirs. They wept for the loss of their friend. They wept for the children she would never have, that is, the very thing that define her worth in society. They entered into her pain. The pain of Jephthah's daughter was not simply her pain alone; it was the pain of the community. They embodied the experience by wearing mourning clothes, tearing their garments, baring body parts, beating their breasts, and weeping.[19] We can imagine Jephthah's

18. Renita Weems, "A Crying Shame (Jephthah's Daughter and the Mourning Women)," in *Just a Sister Away: A Womanist Vision of Women's Relationships in the Bible* (Philadelphia, PA: Innisfree Press, 1988), 58.

19. Barbara Miller, *Tell It On the Mountain: The Daughter of Jephthah in Judges 11* (Collegeville, MN: Liturgical Press, 2005), 88.

daughter and her girlfriends doing this in the hills of Gilead crying, expecting, hoping that God would change God's mind. And yet, God didn't. Perhaps in the space that Jephthah's daughter and her girlfriends created was salvation, freedom, and release.

I'm Free

Jephthah's daughter reminds me that despite being treated or seen as a commodity, I still have value and sacred worth. She teaches me that I have the ability to give voice to my pain. I could scream at the top of my lungs about the unfairness of my fate. I could tell God about my disappointment. I could grieve and not be ashamed. I didn't have to be silent anymore. I could voice what grieves my whole being, what grieves the nation, and what grieves the local community. I could urge others to give voice to their pain. I could urge others to lament. I could urge others to holler. Because I believe when pain is silenced, the pain keeps you captive. I acknowledge that the stained glass brick ceiling exists. However, in spite of it, I'm free. I'm free because I'm not afraid to tell my story. I'm free because I'm not afraid to cry out to God and expect God to respond in my circumstances or the circumstances of my community. I'm free because I'm not afraid to holler and make some noise against the racialized and genderized violence in this country or this denomination. I'm free because I'm not afraid of the consequences of naming my grief. I'm Black. I'm young. I'm woman. I'm grieved. I'm free. Are you?

C h a p t e r   T h r e e

I'M BLACK.
I'M KNEELING TO STAND.

Rodney L. Graves
Senior Pastor, McCabe Roberts Avenue United Methodist Church,
Beaumont, Texas

Growing Up with Racism

After confirmation of her pregnancy, my mother immediately placed her right hand on her womb and prayed: "Oh, bless your Holy Name, Jesus. I worship and adore you. I pray in faith that this child is born healthy. I declare that my child will be extraordinary and not be limited by this world's expectations; and will walk in your ways all the days of his life. I pray that this child whom you created remain safe in a world that can be hateful to our people." My mother spoke power to the fruit of her womb, believing the biblical witness that the right hand symbolized strength. She believed that her child could experience trauma in the womb and after, so she seized the moment with intentionality. Jesus's words spoke to her heart "I came so that they could have life—indeed, so that they could live life to the fullest" (John 10:10), which included her unborn children, the four sisters born after me.

29

When my parents were children attending segregated schools, they always received old, worn textbooks ostensibly no longer good enough for White students. These textbooks often had tape on the corners to keep the books from falling apart. My parents perceived that education was key to advancing in the world; they committed to always have good books in our home. To improve our chance of making it in this world, my parents cultivated our entrepreneurial spirits, adopting W. E. B. DuBois's emphasis on formal education and Booker T. Washington's emphasis on entrepreneurship.

The year before I started elementary school, the Supreme Court ruled in *Brown v. Board of Education* that school segregation was unconstitutional. Slightly before integrating into elementary school, I almost lost my right arm. By repeatedly sticking my hand close to the washing machine wringer, I got my arm caught. My screams brought my strong dad running, who released me from the ferocious grip of the washing machine's rolling pins. Dad rushed me to Johns Hopkins University's hospital. After my dad briefly left the hospital room, the attending nurse stated that it would have been better if my arm had been completely cut off. I never forgot her words, but I naively trusted that she was giving me well-intended medical advice. Yet I should have known otherwise because she touched me as if I were contagiously poison. It took me many years to realize that she was projecting disgust on a defenseless child, nervous about his recovery. Her behavior, while categorically reflective of personal racism, also exhibited institutional racism within the walls of one of the world's most prestigious research hospitals.

While the nearly five-year-old me didn't understand the micro-aggressive significance of the nurse's attack on a child, I did understand what happened to the fourteen-year old-Emmett Till. Both events happened in the summer of 1955. At the time, my entire church and community solemnly mourned this tragedy. Emmett Till's death, exacerbated by the subsequent acquittal of his murderers, indicated that once again, Black lives didn't matter in America. Because a White woman accused Emmett of whistling at her, her family brutally mangled Emmett's body. Years later, she admitted to lying. Perhaps her dying confession ameliorated her tortured soul. But recanting her lie did absolutely nothing to return Emmett or his friends and family to a life of untold possibilities.

Despite a growing awareness of continuing inhumane indignities, I yearned for a closer relationship with Jesus Christ. My eight-year-old self believed there was a place for me in God's kingdom. One Sunday, while engrossed in my dad's preaching, I heard the voice of Jesus calling me to his side. I joined church that day. Jesus Christ desires all to be saved, which is one of the beautiful tenets of biblical Christian faith. As an eight-year-old I realized that genuine Christianity is not exclusive to White people but open to all. Neither the Civil Rights Act of 1964 nor the Voting Rights Act of 1965 had been passed. Although these acts were designed to give equal rights and opened some doors to opportunity, they failed miserably in changing minds, hearts, and wills. Nevertheless, as I grew to understand my calling, I reveled in Jesus Christ's unconditional acceptance and minimized my angst about a world that said I was less than.

The same year that I accepted Christ was also highlighted by the initiation of the Black (formerly Negro) History contests in our church. Enolia P. McMillan, a great educator who later became the first woman president of the NAACP, began these contests. This courageous woman, who secured equal pay for Black teachers in Maryland, was a faithful member of our church. Each year, she gave us a list of names containing Black Americans who achieved much. Her lists included persons who were not well known by the masses. Therefore, we had to creatively and painstakingly research many references to find out who they were, long before web search engines. Mrs. McMillan's contests included prizes. Even participants who didn't win a prize were blessed through laughter by this multigenerational event. Laughter eased the pain of loving a country and a community, which often didn't love us back. And our enlightenment empowered us to deal with the reality that the morning was coming when we would resume the fight to be human.

Many Black families are very intentional about preparing their children for a world institutionally designed for their failure. My dad often said, "Son, you are as good as anyone else, White or Black. You are wonderfully and marvelously made" (cf. Psalm 139:14). I often felt empowered because I, like my dad, was the oldest son in the family. I surmised that my dad felt a special kinship to me. Little did I know, he was also saying the same things to my sisters. What I later realized and respected is that he wanted his daughters to be as prepared as his son. He realized that both his son and daughters would be treated unfairly because of the color of their skin. Black males and females go through some of the same horrors and yet, they experience different horrors. Daddy was committed to making sure that all his children were empowered to exceed societal limits. My dad spoke God's Word into our lives because it could defeat the lethal weapons of the enemy who comes to "steal, kill, and destroy" (John 10:10). Dad knew, "We aren't fighting against human enemies but against rulers, authorities, forces of cosmic darkness, and spiritual powers of evil in the heavens" (Ephesians 6:12).

During my early teen years, I had both a major disappointment and celebration related to Martin Luther King Jr. On the day that Rev. King gave his famous "I Have a Dream" speech, I missed it because I was playing basketball, and my dad left without me. Through my disappointment, I learned to honor time, be responsible, and pay attention.

My disappointment was lessened when Vernon Johns (Rev. King's predecessor at Dexter Avenue Baptist Church) came to our home. My dad invited Johns so he could pick his brain about pastoring, administration, and community engagement. I was not only proud of my dad's ingenuity and humility but also his seeking wise counsel, as urged by Proverbs.

At age fifteen, I attended a prestigious public high school: Baltimore City College. During my three years, I participated in many extracurricular activities but primarily focused on academics. In the eleventh grade, I took an aptitude test that indicated that I had strong mathematical acumen. The guidance counselor indicated that I might become "an accounting clerk or bookkeeper, but Negroes were not smart enough to become accountants." I never forgot those disparaging remarks. These mean-spirited words motivated me to become a certified public accountant (CPA) licensed in both California (1979) and Texas (1982). I was also a cofounder/owner of a Texas-based accounting practice, which was once the largest Black-owned CPA firm in a five-state area (Texas, Arkansas, Louisiana, Oklahoma, and New Mexico). Our faith empowers us to deal with moments of prejudice and institutional racism. Recall Joseph who was speaking to his selfish brothers: "You planned something bad for me, but God produced something good from it" (Gen 50:20). Family conflict and racial strife each have a taproot in selfish desires.

Two sudden deaths rocked me to the core before I graduated from high school. Both persons lived the Great Commandment to fully love God, humankind, and oneself. In January 1968, my baby sister Robin died. Robin was an angel who taught our family how to love more deeply. Robin was born with Down syndrome during a time when people like her were called Mongoloid idiots. Yet Robin intuitively understood and shared love in a way that changed our home. Yes, we were loving before she was born, but afterward, she effortlessly took us to unimaginable levels of closeness. Each morning, Robin would try to awaken us, first by calling our names, accompanied by a gentle nudge, and then with a kiss on the forehead. These sublime moments drew me closer to our creator. When Robin died, I felt indifferent even about my imminent graduation.

Three months later, Martin Luther King Jr. was assassinated. Our family's grieving was interrupted by riots. Two years earlier while advocating nonviolence, King contended that "riots are the language of the unheard." King understood that riots resulted from the lack of progress in social justice, but he remained committed to nonviolent protests. Because of that principle, my father took me with him to the streets to help quell the violent havoc. We witnessed rioting, looting, and property damage by a people angry that their nonviolent leader was violently killed. We prayed before going out in the dark streets toward the fire-lit commercial center. The dangerous walk through the neighborhood felt safe only because I was with my brave, strong, spiritually grounded father. Nevertheless, we continuously prayed while engaging people who felt unheard and were not in the mood to listen; some did listen and others ignored us, but no one harmed us. The community knew my dad and respected his motives. We literally walked by faith, leaning on the Lord.

A Prodigal Son: I'm (Not) Christian.

At age seventeen, I entered Howard University during the turbulent late 1960s. I avidly supported King's nonviolent protest methods. At Howard University, I was exposed to the Black Power movement, which espoused the beauty of Blackness and Malcolm X's alternative: "freedom by any means necessary." While learning a lot about racial oppression in both America and apartheid South Africa, I began to explore faith questions. Classwork in the humanities opened my mind to different ways of looking at spirituality and religion. After I read a book on Deism, I retained my belief in God, but perceived organized religion as unnecessary. Then I read that Karl Marx called religion "the opiate of the people." While I didn't embrace communism, I did question the existence of God. Initially, I became an agnostic, doubting God's existence, but not totally discounting it. I later believed that an agnostic was an atheist who held an insurance policy, just in case he was wrong. I concluded that agnosticism was cowardly, so I embraced atheism.

I embraced atheism because I could not reconcile a good God with all the ugliness in the world. I was particularly concerned about the ugliness of racism, poverty, starvation, greed, violence, and sickness. I surmised that either God was dead, asleep, or didn't give a damn. Perhaps, God was even a jokester playing with our lives and laughing at our craziness. By looking with a distorted lens at the church, I saw unfaithful, petty, hypocritical, selfish, hateful, unforgiving, judgmental, lying people.

I wanted nothing to do with either God or church. My father, mother, and family freaked. They formed prayer groups at church, where people were constantly praying for my return to the faith. They were hoping that I would behave like the prodigal son and "come to myself and return to my father's house." My family and God's people were kneeling, hoping that their prayers would get me to stand up for Jesus.

I rejected the church, in part, because of its perpetuation of and acquiescence to racist biblical misinterpretations. Perhaps the worst interpretations have been ascribed to Noah's curse found in Genesis 9:21-27. Noah had three sons, purportedly representing the major races of the world. Noah's youngest son, Ham (representing Black people), sees his drunken father naked and tells his two brothers. His two brothers cover up their dad, who eventually sobers up and curses Ham's son, Canaan. Noah indicates that Canaan will be a slave and Japheth (representing White people) will take over the land.

Based on their misinterpretation of these passages, White supremacists proselytize that God commanded Black people to be slaves, perennially childlike, and innately inferior in every way, especially intellectually. In other words, when "God created humanity in God's own image" (Gen 1:27), this didn't include Black people.

Furthermore, the universal Church's failure to refute this overt racist dogma fosters its acceptance. And the universal Church enables this atrocity by teaching that Ham (although the text says Ham's son, Canaan) would serve the descendants of the other brothers. Basic critical thinking reveals the obvious bias of White supremacists, and every teacher in the church should refute these views by taking an antiracist stance:

1. Noah was drunk and naked. What in the passage indicates that God honored the curse of one who was not in a consecrated state but rather recovering from alcohol abuse?

2. Noah's so-called curse is directed at Ham's son, Canaan, who was not involved. Why curse Canaan and not Ham? To believe and teach that the curse is divine will represents proof-texting at its worse.

3. Ham didn't walk in on a drunk, naked father intending to dishonor Noah. There is no evidence that Ham mocked his father. Ham, the younger son, honored tradition by deferring to his older siblings about what to do.

4. Finally, I could not correlate how White hatred called Jews inferior, and yet allow one to still "worship" the loving, Jewish Jesus. I questioned how intellectual superiority insulates racists from this contradiction.

Four years after graduating from Howard University with a combined degree in accounting and economics, I left my Baltimore hometown. I left to get my CPA license in California because it afforded the opportunity for reciprocity in other states. Ashamedly, I had a less than honorable reason for leaving. I realized that I didn't want to lose my professional status because I enjoyed smoking marijuana; in California, possessing less than an ounce was a misdemeanor that would not derail my career. As I prepared to leave, my dad called an incredulous family into a prayer circle. By showing the wisdom of the prodigal son's father, he released me, believing that I would one day come to myself and return to the faith of my ancestors.

While driving to California across Middle America in a Datsun 260Z sports car, I had many crazy experiences. I realized that my foreign car and Blackness offended Middle America, but thank God, they didn't know what I was carrying. I had some high-quality marijuana (Panama Red). I smoked some and even shared with a White, hitchhiking hippie. I finally ran out of the weed. While driving up a ten-mile-long mountainous highway in Salt Lake City (of all places), something happened. I was overcome with a strong divine presence that I knew was the God of my people. I immediately knew that the saints' prayers were working on me. I was so overwhelmed that I cried and begged God to forgive me for my unbelief.

Coming Home: I'm Methodist.

My Methodist tradition teaches me that it was the prevenient grace of God at work in my life. Prevenient means "that grace which comes before"; God had been pursuing me (prevenient grace) and now I received God's acceptance (justifying grace). While driving up that mountain road, I came back to God but not the church. However, these words no longer applied to me: "Fools say in their hearts, 'There is no God'" (Ps 14:1). I felt relieved, because my well-being had been restored, and I knew that my family believed "the prayer of the righteous person is powerful in what it can achieve" (Ja 5:16).

I didn't return to the Lord's church until eight years later. I was in an emotionally abusive relationship, which drove me to my knees. In my pain, I longed for a return to a faith community. A neighbor invited me to Windsor Village United Methodist Church. I enjoyed the worship, and the expressive hospitality helped heal some of my woundedness. I was initially uncomfortable when I saw the word *catholic* in the Apostles' Creed (not used in my early Baptist upbringing). But Pastor Kirbyjon H. Caldwell anticipated that some would disconnect, so he explained it to us saying "the word *catholic* refers to God's universal church, not to the Roman Catholic Church, even though we have utmost love and respect for the Roman Catholic Church." I felt some relief in agreement. More important, I felt help, healing, and hope for the first time in what felt like forever. As it's been said before, "Pain will teach you what pride won't let you learn."

Then, I noticed Pastor Caldwell talked a lot about some man named John Wesley. I surmised he was the unwitting founder of Methodism. Wesley advanced the idea that "means of grace" included prayer. Before the prayer altar call, Pastor Caldwell would initiate a call-and-response phrase, which began loud and descended to a whisper: "MUCH PRAYER-MUCH POWER, Little Prayer-Little Power, and no prayer-no power." I realized that prayer is not merely having a microwave conversation with God at bedtime, nor is it merely seeking *God* to fix my life or give me things. Prayer is communion with God and necessary to grow spiritually. John Wesley considered it a path into "sanctifying grace," which means that by the power of the Holy Spirit, one grows in grace (divine love). I became so thirsty for more, that, though I was a night owl, I attended a daily 6:00 a.m. prayer-power small group. In my unhealthy relationship, I had been on my knees having a pity party, wishing for the pain to end. Now I was kneeling in prayer, so that I could stand on God's Word and walk again with God's deliverance.

On Super Bowl Sunday 1985, the pastor preached a sermon titled "Hallelujah Anyhow." "Hallelujah" is the highest praise because it means "celebrate God." I felt the Holy Spirit breaking the chains wrapped around my whole being. My thoughts, emotions, and desires began to embrace life. I joined the church that day, but more important, I formalized my covenant with Jesus Christ. After church, I gave my body the same freedom that my heart and mind had received: I left a house that never was a home, and unlike Lot's wife, I never looked back. The toxicity in that relationship drove me to my knees, whereas Jesus Christ "picked me up and turned me around. Hallelujah, Hallelujah, Jesus saves." But I also sought and received good therapy, because I knew that I couldn't be spiritually mature and emotionally unhealthy.

After years of interior work with professionals and enrichment groups, I continued to pray for a mate, and God set the stage. At the time, I was pastoring in Richmond, Virginia, but had returned for a visit to Houston, Texas. Through some dear friends, I met Ava over the telephone. I initially talked to her on April 15—a date that had a lot of significance for me when I was a CPA. We talked and before hanging up she asked, "Can we pray"? No one had ever asked that before, and neither had I: this stunned me and piqued my interest. We even talked about our commitment to sexual abstinence. Even a phone meeting with another adult practicing abstinence was refreshing because that conversation often got awkward with dating partners. On the birthday (seven days later) of the friend who connected us, I stated to Ava, "I believe that the Lord told me that you are going to be my wife." Ava said, "What took you so long?" We committed to get married—sight unseen. Months later when I got off the airplane in Houston, I was magnetically drawn to this glowingly beautiful woman who simultaneously locked in on me. Nine months later, we got married. That happened nearly twenty-four years ago. Beautiful story, but we, too, have had to kneel to stand.

In our previous pastoral appointment, we began each year with a focused month of prayer and fasting. Through our communal spiritual discipline, God sent a great opportunity. I was approached by a phenomenally successful entrepreneur needing my support. He desired to build two luxurious affordable apartment complexes behind the church. "Scott" (a pseudonym) stated that he sought tax credits but needed community (legislators and neighborhood associations) support. These community leaders told Scott that "if Pastor Graves approved, they would support it." After listening to Scott's pitch, I said, "Scott, White people come to our neighborhoods all the time and after they leave, they're the only ones who benefited or made money. I will not help unless you promise to hire persons from the neighborhood and use area small businesses when possible." Scott said, "Pastor Graves, I know that you don't know me, but I'm a man of my word and will do everything you asked." Scott did more than I asked. He replaced the community's septic tank with a $5 million wastewater system. Scott placed a $40,000 irrigation system at the neighborhood library. The apartment buildings were first-class with a forty-seat movie theater, state-of-the-art business center, game room, panoramic view of downtown Houston, and many other amenities. This housing was a tremendous upgrade for the residents, who never dreamed that they would be able to live affordably this way. Participating in Wesley's means of grace, we knelt to stand and witnessed a mighty move of *God* benefiting the least, lost, and last.

In our current pastoral appointment, we continue to pray and fast. Several times, our foci have been on the seven *F*s:

1. Faith,

2. Family,

3. Friends,

4. Foes,

5. Finances,

6. Food, and

7. Fitness.

We expanded our definition of "Family and Friends" to include the youth and children of our city. Through Ava's outreach, we collaborated with IEA (Inspire, Encourage, and Achieve)—a youth at-risk program using Mirian Wright Edelman's Freedom School concepts. We also collaborated with HYPE Freedom School and the Texas Annual Conference of The UMC to work with at-risk children.[20]

I'm Black. I'm Christian. I'm Methodist. These identities inform my witness of kneeling to stand. Kneeling quiets my thoughts, emotions, and desires. Kneeling centers my life. Kneeling guides my feet so that I can stand for Christ. Kneeling is bowing down in God's presence so that I can stand up to anything opposing God's purpose for my life. Jesus knelt in the garden of Gethsemane so that he could stand before death, with the passionate blend of humility and holy boldness. Many people have knelt before engaging in nonviolent protests for the right to be human. Many have knelt as a sign of submission to God and opposition to oppression: Martin Luther King Jr. and his followers knelt, and so have professional athletes.

Martin Luther King Jr. stood on this nation's principles of life, liberty, and the pursuit of happiness—as well as the right to

---

20. These and other life-transforming ministries are documented in my DMin thesis at Asbury Theological Seminary: *Breaking Generational Poverty through Collaborative Efforts.*

peacefully protest. Engaging in the principles of America's found-ers is both a call and challenge to our great nation to live out its covenants. The call reflects a love that has survived dehumaniza-tion, exploitation, and violence to our bodies. The challenge can only be met through divine intervention and human repentance.

So that at the name of Jesus everyone
    in heaven, on earth, and under the earth might bow
    and every tongue confess
        that "Jesus Christ is Lord, to the glory of God the Father.
                                  (Phil 2:10-11)

I'M BLACK. I'VE SEEN.
I REMAIN.

Lillian C. Smith

Senior Pastor, Cheverly United Methodist Church, Hyattsville, Maryland

> A charge to keep, I have,
> a God to glorify,
> a never dying soul to save,
> and fit it for the sky.
> —Charles Wesley, "A Charge to Keep I Have," 1762

The United Methodist Church experienced steep decline since the merger of The Evangelical United Brethren and Methodist churches in 1968. When the denomination formed fifty years ago, during the civil rights era that involved many Black Methodists, we did not anticipate how much African American United Methodist churches would struggle to exist in 2020. We've gone high and low with civil rights reform, but racism is surging in American society, within the Christian community, and in the denomination I love. Sunday morning worship, in numerous UM congregations, remains highly segregated. In a time when leaders in our society are increasingly diverse, ethnically and in gender, cross-cultural appointments often result in challenging relationships for both pastor and congregation. The creation and cultivation of multicultural United Methodist fellowships can be a struggle.

As an African American, I've asked myself many times:

- Why am I a Methodist?

- Why have I stayed in The United Methodist Church?

- Why do I stay when many of my family members have left?

- Why have I stayed when many of the young people I taught in various congregations left The United Methodist Church to find other Christian faith traditions?

- Has God forgotten Black people in The United Methodist Church or have we lost our way?

To say that The United Methodist Church is the only ministry I experienced would be inacurate. God has used numerous ecumenical connections to bless and influence me, including nondenominational, Presbyterian, Pentecostal, Charismatic, and Baptist. Yet my spiritual journey remains rooted in The United Methodist Church.

As a cradle Methodist, I was born during the last few years of the Central Jurisdiction. Formed in 1939, the Central Jurisdiction was the racially defined jurisdiction comprising African American Methodist Episcopal congregations. This grouping of Black congregations allowed the merging denominations— Methodist Protestant, Methodist Episcopal Church, South, and the Methodist Episcopal Church—to neatly address the problem of Negro Methodists in a country that eschewed racial parity and justice for African Americans. Even though early Methodism condemned slavery and required Methodist Episcopal clergy and laity to release slaves or be expelled, racism was a constant problem among the people called Methodist. The issue of slavery split The Methodist Episcopal Church in 1849. In 1968, at the merger of The Evangelical United Brethren Church and The Methodist Church, the segregated Central Jurisdiction was dissolved.

Though a reflection of God's multicolored family, the Black presence (described as Negro) within American Methodism presented a problem in a racially charged society. My parents and grandparents were a part of the Central Jurisdiction. The late bishop Charles Golden baptized me during a gathering of the Central Jurisdiction College of Bishops. While in a segregated reality, they enjoyed vibrant and active congregations that ministered healing to hurting communities. These congregations and conferences started colleges and developed strong leaders that influenced and uplifted their communities. It is into this reality, though flawed, that I was born.

My Methodist Ancestors

I began life as a Christian in The Methodist Church because of my parents. I remain a Christian in The United Methodist body of the faith because God called and assigned me to this mission field. God has not released me to leave. In one regard, my assignment, and that of other African Americans who remain active in ministry within The United Methodist Church, is defined by John Wesley. In her essay "Spreading Scriptural Holiness: Theology and Practices of Early Methodism for the Contemporary Church," Laceye Warner describes the purpose that keeps me in. She wrote: "In the 'Large' Minutes, John Wesley summarized his understanding of Methodism's purpose:

'What may we reasonably believe to be God's design in raising up the Preachers called Methodists? A. To reform the nation and, in particular, the Church; to spread scriptural holiness over the land.'"[21] Ministering to the entire community and parish to which I'm assigned, as well as leading the ministry, in spiritual renewal and discipleship, has been my call in each of the settings I've served.[22] The community and UMC need revival now as much as the Church of England needed it during Wesley's time.

Kinship identity also keeps me grounded in The United Methodist Church. The roll call of family members in the Methodist faith community include Rosetta and Francis Asbury Webb, Leah and Edward Poole, Eula and Charli Smith, Lillie and Hayward Webb, and Doris and C. Jasper Smith. Both my parents, Doris Webb Smith and Charli Jasper Smith, were Methodists. On my father's side, we can trace participation in the Methodist Episcopal branch back to his maternal, great-grandfather, Miles Newman, born either in 1801 or 1803. A historical marker and oral history record that Miles Newman donated property on which McBee United Methodist Church was built in McBee, South Carolina.[23] The late United Methodist bishop Ernest Newman and UM pastor, South Carolina state senator, and civil rights activist, the Rev. I. DeQuincey Newman both are related to Miles Newman. The family commitment to Methodist ministry is strong. My father,

21. Laceye Warner, "Spreading Scriptural Holiness: Theology and Practices of Early Methodism for the Contemporary Church," *The Asbury Journal 63, no. 1* (2008): 115, assessed September 11, 2020, https://core.ac.uk/download/pdf/155818541.pdf.
22. These include serving as pastor of local congregations, campus minister; director—Campus Ministry Section, General Board of Higher Education and Ministry; and associate general secretary—Young People's Division, General Board of Discipleship, and director—Connectional Ministries.
23. Sharon O'Neill, Johnson/McQueen/McFarland family historian confirmed the Miles Newman history. September 7, 2020.

the Reverend C. Jasper Smith, who served as a pastor and district superintendent in the South Carolina Conference, helped build the church building of Mt. Elon UMC, also in South Carolina.

On my mother's side, both her parents were Methodists. Her mother, Lillie Poole Webb, was a Methodist from the Eastern Shore of Virginia and her father, Hayward T. Webb, hailed from the Eastern Shore of Maryland. Her paternal grandfather was named Francis Asbury Webb. Methodism is a part of who I am as a Christian.

Each of my parents was trained at Methodist-related or Methodist-birthed schools. My father attended Claflin College in South Carolina and Gammon Theological Seminary in Atlanta, Georgia. My mother attended Morgan State College. Though now a state university, it started in 1867 as Centenary Biblical Institute, to train men for ministry and then prepare men and women to teach. Birthed at Sharp Street Methodist Church, the school was started by the Baltimore Annual Conference, a part of the Central Jurisdiction. My mother's parents, Lillie and Hayward, met when they attended the Princess Anne Academy of Morgan College, now known as University of Maryland Eastern Shore. Hayward later attended Meharry Medical College, a United Methodist–related school in Nashville, Tennessee. Methodism was the womb and community to which my ancestors were born.

In a racist society, The Methodist Church provided a place of faith, strength, love, and solace for Black people. My mother recalled memories of her family going to Tindley Temple, in Philadelphia, for the meeting of the Delaware Annual Conference. The Delaware Conference, part of the Central Jurisdiction, would meet at Tindley Temple. She shared how the time was exciting. The sanctuary, which can seat about four thousand people, would be full and the worship was vibrant. Numerous writings recount the power of the Holy Spirit that was present in that congregation in its earlier days. It was said that it seemed as if the Holy Spirit was downloading messages to the preachers as they brought the Word of God. Tindley Temple provided much for the community amid the Great Depression, including opening its sanctuary to provide a place for people to sleep at night, and meals in its soup kitchen. I would later serve that congregation as pastor. Though the building was filled with memories of a by-gone era, the significantly smaller congregation I served struggled to define God's call in a new time in a changing neighborhood.

How Methodism Attracted Black Participants

Why was early Methodism so attractive to enslaved and free African Americans? The Methodist approach to the faith preached of the saving grace of God for all humanity, in all walks of life, free, enslaved, Black, White, Native American, people of all colors. Slavery was initially opposed in preaching. At its core, Methodism was an expression of the Christian faith that welcomed and embraced the movement of the Holy Spirit and spontaneity. It was easily adaptable to the worship expression of the Black culture, and it communicated God's love for all.

In the essay "Black People in the Methodist Church: A Fierce Fidelity to a Church for Whom Grace Is Central," William B. Mc-Clain wrote about the affinity of Blacks to The Methodist Episcopal Church as he described his home congregation, Sweet Home Methodist Episcopal Church. Located in Gadsden, Alabama, Sweet Home Methodist Episcopal Church began seven years after slavery ended. McClain explained that it was "connected to the northern branch, the one that believed that slavery was wrong, the one that taught that grace was free and open and available to all, even to those who were in legal bondage."[24]

Many descendants of Black Methodist believers, in the United Methodist branch, remain loyal to a church that has not always lived out its true calling and precepts. Others left The Methodist/ Methodist Episcopal Church but remained connected to the Wesleyan form of ministry. Even though Bishop Richard Allen left The Methodist Episcopal Church to start the African Methodist Episcopal Church, he remained a Methodist until he died. Ordained by Bishop Francis Asbury as the first Black deacon in The Methodist Episcopal Church, Allen remained a Methodist, even after forced to leave the prayer railing at Old St. George's Methodist Episcopal Church, so that Whites could occupy that space. Allen remained Methodist even after White church leadership did everything within their legal power to stop the new faith community of Bethel from worshipping, by trying to control when services would be held, by attempting to only allowing a White pastor from Old St. George's to preach. Allen stayed even after raising funds to purchase back the property and building after the White establishment wrangled it out of the new Black congregation's hands. The Methodist message of saving grace is strong and relevant even when humanity falters in living it out.

It was this message of God's good news, shared by the people and congregation of Asbury United Methodist Church, located in downtown Washington, DC, that molded generations of young

24. William B. McClain, "Black People in the Methodist Church: A Fierce Fidelity to a Church for Whom Grace Is Central." *Methodist History* 54, no. 1 (October 2015) 81; http://archives.gcah.org/bitstream/handle/10516/9811/Methodist -History-2015-10-McClain.pdf?sequence=1, accessed October 2, 2020..

Black people into leaders. At Asbury, I was converted to a saving knowledge of Jesus Christ. Motivational speakers (Willie Jolley, actor Michael Genet) and countless preachers (Steve Tillet, Carol Sloan, Ronald Bess, and Lillian Smith) were impacted by the ministry of people like Grace Bradford, Bishop Marcus Matthews, and Mildred Hill, who fulfilled the call of making disciples of Jesus Christ for the transformation of the world. This congregation nurtured and developed numerous individuals to lead. The list of the congregation's leadership and ministry beneficiaries is too long to list them all. Even Asbury, a historic African American congregation, made racial diversity an expectation. People of other cultures and colors were always welcome to participate as guests or members. Curt Campaign, an Anglo male, served as an associate pastor during my childhood.

My ministry and leadership were developed in the protective womb of this community of Black Christian believers who worked to equip its young people with faith and skills needed to withstand and overcome society's racism. They taught us that we are God's children. They taught us we could do anything with God's help. They taught us that nothing is impossible with God. As is true with many Methodist congregations, many of Asbury's members or constituents were community leaders who actively worked vocationally to improve the lives of others. Examples include Althea Simmons, lawyer and civil rights activist with the NAACP, and Clive Callendar, professor of transplant surgery at Howard University Hospital. This commitment to resist and change a racist world was also the case at Sharp Street Methodist Church in Baltimore, where abolitionist Frederick Douglass was briefly a member and lay preacher.

Why Black Participants Left

I remain, not because the people called Methodist are perfect, but because God's grace and the message of salvation is what drives us to serve God's mission. I remain because the mission is just as pressing today as it was centuries ago. I remain because Blacks have a place in this Methodist movement just as they have a place in this nation. Blacks have long been a part of Methodism. An enslaved woman, Annie Sweitzer, was an active member of the first Methodist society, which met in the home of John Evans, now at the Strawbridge Shrine, in New Windsor, Maryland, in or around 1763.[25] Blacks helped to build and develop what is now The United Methodist Church; its Christian witness, outreach, assets, and legacy. I have no expectation of going someplace else, unless God tells me to move on. It is my belief that I will be a part of Methodism until I take my last breath.

Even though the Methodists missed the mark many times with Black participants, it did and continues to value ethnic and cultural diversity in practice. The United Methodist denominational board and agencies have long demonstrated a commitment to ethnic and cultural diversity among board/commission members and staff. Sometimes it was actualized better than other times, but the commitment is there.

But what causes Black participants to leave the denomination? Why has the United Methodist denomination lost its attraction to African Americans? In some instances, congregations became so wedded to the past that they didn't allow the Holy Spirit to move in a way that would continue to engage and transform

25. "Methodist History: Slave Welcomed as One of First Members" https://www.umc.org/en/content/methodist-history-slave-welcomed-as-one-of-first-members, accessed September 9, 2020.

subsequent generations of people. Whereas, fifty years ago, many Black United Methodist congregations were leading at the forefront of societal change, many adapted and became parked in the past. Imagine my surprise when I learned that my home congregation had a gospel choir before Howard University did. What? When I was growing up, the church choirs sang spirituals but not what we now call Black gospel music. There was no gospel choir when I grew up. Every now and then stories were recounted about a gentleman from the South who would either shout or run when the Holy Spirit moved him. Really? That was not my experience. I had at times heard at my home church and elsewhere that "we don't say amen here." Perhaps there developed an understanding, in some Black churches, that to be a good United Methodist one must repress cultural nuances of the Black worship experience.

The generational divide exists in all cultures. In Black congregations that refused to embrace God's move through younger generations, the result was a mass exodus of young people. Examples of this include conversations between generations about music: "We do not sing that kind of music here." Or "We don't say 'amen' here." An unwillingness to adapt to the new thing God is doing and a loss of urgency to relate a relevant message and expression of the gospel to the community meant that many younger generations left, many to go to other churches that embraced an evolving Black culture.

It is often said that when White America catches a cold, Black America gets pneumonia. That is true even in the realms of Christian ministry. As the members of The United Methodist Church became more middle class and affluent, the move and power of the Holy Spirit waned. The movement to make disciples eventually changed to focus more on maintaining what was in existence.

Combine the factors of (1) what it means to be United Methodist and a middle-class or affluent person, with (2) what it means to be a Black and Methodist person, and we see a diminishing result. Did the Holy Spirit leave? No. But our lack of openness to being used by the Holy Spirit quenched its movement.

In numerous Black United Methodist churches, it appears as if people have forgotten or forfeited their rich spiritual heritage. For many, worship is parked in the nineteenth or twentieth centuries. In many congregations, the mission to reach others with the powerful good news and amazing grace has transformed to focus internally on the needs of the members and to maintain their legacy and sometimes that of the building. Intentional discipleship through Bible study, prayer meetings, and small groups has become a dormant possibility in many Black UM congregations. Worship wars continue about which music to sing, how to worship, and what new ministry efforts to begin. Again, when the greater community catches a cold, the Black community gets pneumonia. The consequences are detrimental to the Black community. People of African descent in America would have been destroyed had the Lord not been on their side.

The suppression of cultural worship expressions can be a challenging situation to African American United Methodist churches. Let's concede that present-day Methodists are characteristically reserved and not demonstrative in worship. It can be said that Methodists are not very expressive. That has not always been the case. In the earliest days of Methodism, God's Spirit moved mightily. In John Wesley's lifetime, it was reported that when he preached, conviction of the Holy Spirit would manifest mightily and people would subsequently fall out, experience the shakes, and experience a holy laughter. Many people were reportedly "slain in the Spirit." In one instance, John Wesley recounts the following incident in his journal on Thursday, April 25, 1739, "Immediately one, and another, and another sunk to the earth: they dropped as if they were thunderstruck. One of them cried aloud."[26] His journals also record him praying to expel demons.[27]

The openness to free expression in worship may have been an additional reason that free and enslaved Africans were attracted to the Methodists in America. That free expression continued into the next century. In the 1800s, Methodists were derided with the label "Shouting Methodists." Methodists were initially known for their enthusiasm. American evangelist, pastor, and teacher R. A. Torrey, knew well the reputation of Shouting Methodists. Torrey (1856–1928) wrote the following to describe an encounter he had with the Holy Spirit: "Sometime after this experience (I do not recall just how long after), while sitting in my room one day . . . suddenly . . . I found myself shouting (I was not brought up to shout and I'm not of a shouting temperament, but I shouted like the loudest shouting Methodist), Glory to God, glory to God, glory to God,' and I could not stop."[28]

Torrey's experience was not an anomaly. Songs were written about those enthusiastic Methodists. The song "The Methodist" is an example about shouting Methodists. Here,

---

26.   John Wesley, *Wesley His Own Historian,* Making of America (MOA) Digital Library, accessed September 11, 2020, https://quod.lib.umich.edu/m/moa/AGV 9079.0001.001?rgn=main;view=fulltex.

27.   John Wesley, *Journal of John Wesley,* "A Terrible Sight," Christian Classics Ethereal Library, accessed September 12, 2020, https://ccel.org/ccel/wesley /journal/journal.vi.iii.xii.html.

28.   R. A. Torrey, "Evangelism, Revival and Healing (n.p.: Healing and Revival Press, 2005), accessed September 9, 2020, https://healingandrevival.com/BioRA Torrey.htm.

the lyrics from Stith Mead's 1807 Methodist Songbook support Torrey's insight.[29]

> The World, the Devil, and Tom Paine
> Have try'd their force, but all in vain.
> They can't prevail, the reason is,
> The Lord defends the Methodist.
> They pray, they sing, they preach the best,
> And do the Devil most molest.
> If Satan had his vicious way,
> He'd kill and damn them all today.
> They are despised by Satan's train,
> Because they shout and preach so plain.
> I'm bound to march in endless bliss,
> And die a shouting Methodist.

Much has changed from its early days. The move and power of the Holy Spirit has been quenched. The Holy Spirit is still moving. The Holy Spirit will not force any of us to do anything yet awaits our invitation to move freely in our personal and corporate lives to bring about God's reign.

So it seems many of the people called Methodist, in this instance numerous Black United Methodists, have forgotten or forfeited their spiritual heritage. While we may have forgotten or discarded it, many others, outside the denomination, are remembering and recovering the insights from the movement of the Holy Spirit within the early moves of Methodism. Almost daily, numerous television shows host conversations of people who discuss the strength of John Wesley's preaching and discipleship

---

29. Winthrop S. Hudson, "Shouting Methodists," *Thunderstruck: A Truck Stop for the Soul,* http://thunderstruck.org/revivalflames-shout-htm/, accessed September 9, 2020.

model. On one religious show Mario Murillo explained how God used John Wesley to transform England. England was in a time of serious moral decay. Murillo shared,

> John Wesley began preaching in the slums . . . and one in every 7 buildings in London at that time was a house of prostitution. . . . And more people were going to seances than to the Church of England. Charles Dickens said "here is Paris in a blood bath and London is not." A newspaper asked Dickens what is the difference? Dickens replied, "the preaching of John Wesley."[30]

My hope and prayer is that God will still use Blacks in the entire denomination to touch people with the transforming love of Jesus Christ. To do that, we must be open and obedient to the Holy Spirit. When we do, mighty things happen. This has been the case in many ministries.

Throughout the years, numerous Black Methodist/United Methodist congregations embraced and flowed with further waves of the Holy Spirit. Some of those congregations included Philadelphia—Tindley Temple; Atlanta—Ben Hill, Cascade, Central; Houston—Windsor Village and St. John's Downtown; Washington, DC—Emory Fellowship.

John Wesley found himself in an English society that was fraught with moral decay, spiritual malaise, poverty, and great change. John Wesley remained an Anglican priest even as the ministry implemented a more methodical way of preaching salvation and discipling people to transform the nation and change the world.

The Methodist Church began at the same time the American nation began. As the church and the country expanded, both

30. Mario Murillo, "Exposing Satan's End Time Strategy," interview by Larry Sparks, https://www.youtube.com/watch?v=Efl_Vok_r98.

struggled with the country's original sin of racism. The existence of the Central Jurisdiction in The Methodist Church during the Jim Crow period in the nation is a key example of racism. Efforts continue to confront racism. In response to numerous killings of young African American men, a number of leaders challenged the people and congregations of the Northeastern Jurisdiction to address racism and White privilege, individually and structurally; to acknowledge that Black Lives and the lives of all people of color matter; review the number of Blacks and to "study the impact of structural and institutional racism on Black people, in particular, the closing of Black churches and the impact of the ordination process upon the number of persons interested in ordained ministry."[31]

The Methodist message and expression of the gospel is just as relevant now as it was in the eighteenth century. Now, more than ever, the United States needs Jesus. This nation and our world is in turmoil. After the on-camera killing of George Floyd by a Minneapolis, Minnesota, police officer, protests, most of which have been peaceful and some violent, are still taking place in various cities. Some cities were on fire. The upheaval of the COVID-19 pandemic and virulent racism, in the midst of a contentious election year, threw this nation into a spiral that it can't escape without God. The United Methodist Church also needs a new fire of revival, as it prepares for another split over the issue of same-gender marriage and expression of human sexuality.

---

31. Resolution: A Call to Action to the Northeastern Jurisdiction and Its College of Bishops https://www.epaumc.org/wp-content/uploads/2016/07/Black-ChurchConcernsCalltoActionNEJ.pdf, accessed September 9, 2020.

John Wesley brought revival to his nation and the Anglican Church. He remained an Anglican priest until his dying day. His calls for scriptural holiness and social holiness, reformed Great Britain and spread across the world. The need for revival and healing is no less urgent for this nation and for the people of African descent in the United States and throughout The United Methodist Church. The people called Methodist still offer a relevant understanding of the gospel to share with a racially torn nation. Salvation is for all. Racism is sin. God loves everyone.

Chapter Five

I'M BLACK. I'M METHODIST. I'M FIGHTING FOR RACIAL RECONCILIATION.

Erin Beasley

Associate Pastor, Germantown United Methodist Church,

Germantown, Tennessee

In a Black Church and a White School

I grew up in a Mississippi beach town where diversity and racial division coexisted. When looking back at my childhood, it's clear to me now that I lived what W. E. B. DuBois would call a life of double consciousness. My schools were diverse, but I found myself placed in classes that were predominantly White. Several of my close friends were White. My experience of the church was quite different because my closest friends were Black. I was raised in my father's predominantly Black United Methodist congregation. I saw the beauty in maintaining friendships amid the two very different worlds but wondered what would happen one day if my two worlds became one. I longed for this. I imagined what my Black friends might think of my White friends, and vice versa. Would they hit it off? Would they enjoy each other's company just as much as I enjoyed theirs? My dream came true at my tenth birthday party in 1998. I invited my White friends from school and my Black friends from church to celebrate with me. I will never forget the joy of that day. My two worlds met and had a party. It was magical. I felt complete and fulfilled by that union.

While growing up, I saw diversity in many places except in the church. This dynamic led me to believe that church wasn't the place for racial diversity. I was so wrapped up in the world that nurtured me to the point where I didn't realize I was a part of a racially segregated institution. Worshipping among Black brothers and sisters was life giving. It was safe. It was a social norm that I felt no need to challenge, even while maintaining friendships with White children from school. This was simply the way things were supposed to be. It's interesting how readily I accepted this as a child. No one ever told me that the church wasn't the place for diversity, but I grew to believe it anyway. My father's blooming friendship with a White UMC pastor began the unraveling of my misunderstanding.

A pulpit exchange challenged my developing misconception that people of various racial backgrounds don't worship together. My father's friend served a predominantly White church a few miles away from ours. They desired to cultivate a worship experience that was a better representation of the true body of Christ. A few times a year, my father led worship at his friend's church with our choir. Their church did the same. I'll never forget the first Sunday my father's friend led worship at our church. I wasn't made aware of this amazing, emerging new relationship, so one can imagine my confusion as I gazed upon the preacher, who was clearly not my father, and a choir whose faces didn't resemble the faces I was accustomed to seeing. I was startled initially. It was a sight that I'd never seen before in church, and I didn't know how to make sense of it. After worship, I found my father in his office. I whispered in confusion, "There were White people in our church." He responded with laughter. "Yes, dear. There were. People of all racial backgrounds should worship together." All of a sudden, my confusion seemed silly. After that pivotal moment in my childhood, I wondered why the church was not racially diverse. The years-long pulpit exchange helped me to realize that diversity in worship is indeed possible. I struggled to understand this until much later in my life when I began my ministry journey.

Black Methodists between the Revolution and the Civil War

On April 17, 1960, Martin Luther King Jr. said that Sunday morning is the most segregated hour in America. That was sixty years ago, and despite the strides made toward inclusion and equality since then, King's words still hold true. Perhaps more than ever, our racially homogenous congregations express the need for more diversity, but few are successful in achieving it. The wounds concerning racial division cut terribly deep, and American Christians are at the center of it all. To truly understand why the church is racially divided, we must retrace our Christian footsteps. Retracing our steps enables us to realize the depth of this issue that intensified over the course of several centuries in this country. We've lived through only a few decades of desegregation and intentional strides toward equality. That's a blip in time considering how long slavery and segregation lasted in this country. From the very beginning of the American church, White Christians tried their best to maintain authority not simply over the church but the Christian faith as well. Though White Christians in early America didn't share the same views on social issues, they made an effort to control who had access to the church and the faith itself, from the conversations regarding whether or not slaves should be baptized to the conversations regarding the ordination of Black preachers as elders.

In the time between 1619, when the slave trade began in North America, and 1808, when the importation of slaves to the United States was made illegal, 360,000 Africans who were captured and shackled had already been exposed to or identified with Christianity or Islam. [32] Black exposure to Christianity predated slavery, but White Christians failed to acknowledge this at the time. Africans were perceived as "heathens" and could not have had the capacity to identify with Christianity or any organized religion. This shared notion branded racial prejudice in early American Christianity.

In the early modern world, religious divisions—imposed by European colonists, who distinguished between those who claimed Christ and all others in the heathen world—defined race. European or English meant Christian. African, by contrast, meant heathen, despite the fact that many Africans had been Christianized and that large portions of North Africa and several kingdoms in sub-Saharan Africa had shifted under the sway of Islam. In short, very early on, the categories of religion and race became intertwined in Southern history, each helping to define the other. Religion created race and race thereafter shaped religion. Euro-Americans developed some of the meanings of race in the modern sense. They determined what constituted Whiteness and

---

32. Paul Harvey, *Christianity and Race in the American South* (Chicago: University of Chicago Press, 2016), 17.

Blackness, categories that would long outlive slavery itself. Those categories were fundamentally religious ones.[33]

Many Europeans perceived Africans as irreligious while others saw their customs as "pagan" or "barbaric."[34] Heathenism and Blackness were inextricably linked.[35] As one early commentator put it, "Negroes were 'a people of beastly living, without a God, law, religion, or commonwealth.'"[36] Morgan Godwyn, a minister in seventeenth-century Virginia, expressed that "nothing is more barbarous and contrary to Christianity than their idolatrous dances and revels."[37]

As the African slave population grew to outnumber the colonists, Christian conversion became a point of contention. Others believed Christianity to be an exclusively White religion, while others believe it was their mission to evangelize their slaves. Others naturally feared that Christianity would inspire slaves to revolt, and their fear came to fruition on many occasions. By the early 1700s, "Christianized slaves envisioned a religiously inspired revolution. They insisted that they possessed equal souls and equal rights. They spoke the language of power in courtrooms, in letters to imperial officials, and as a last resort, in rebellions."[38]

The Black Evangelical Awakening, which coincided with the Great Awakening of the eighteenth century, was a time marked by religious enthusiasm. The Awakening resonated with Black slaves because it was a movement marked by profound spiritual expression. This reminded them very much of the "African customs of

---

33. Harvey, *Christianity and Race in the American South*, 19.
34. Harvey, *Christianity and Race in the American South*, 20.
35. Harvey, *Christianity and Race in the American South*, 21.
36. Ibid., 21.
37. Ibid., 21.
38. Harvey, *Christianity and Race in the American South*, 29.

bodily expressiveness in religious rituals."[39] The movement also resonated with Black slaves because revivalists and evangelicals shared a message that moved beyond racial barriers. The Great Awakening gave many Black slaves a sense of identity and belonging that they had never experienced. As a pious desire for Christian knowledge grew among Black people, evangelists took advantage of this appeal.[40] They saw this as an excellent opportunity to fulfill their mission of sharing Christ with all the world. They were moved by the Black awakening but also disturbed by it simultaneously.[41]

The upspring of Black Christianization in this period brought forth more White Christian suspicion and resistance.[42] "The Awakening reinforced the conviction among Whites that spiritual freedom didn't extend to temporal liberation and that religious expressiveness could be embraced but could not be repressed."[43] Some Christian leaders believed that slaves had ulterior motives when converting to Christianity. There was a belief that slaves hoped to gain respect and less discipline from their masters by converting, in addition to their hope for freedom.[44] Over time, even as slaves gained their freedom, the relationship between Black and White Christians deteriorated, though it was never solid from the start.

Methodism began in America initially as an interracial movement, but Blacks were never immune to racism. "The racial prejudices of colonial American society deeply influenced early Ameri-

---

39. Harvey, *Christianity and Race in the American South*, 42.
40. Harvey, *Christianity and Race in the American South*, 44.
41. Harvey, *Christianity and Race in the American South*, 43.
42. Ibid., 43.
43. Harvey, *Christianity and Race in the American South*, 42.
44. Ibid., 42.

can Methodists even as they proclaimed the gospel open to all."[45] By 1774, the Methodists had gained over five hundred free African Americans.[46] They made up at least 25 percent of the movement.[47] There certainly were more persons of African descent within these ranks, but the slaves were omitted from that figure. The Methodist movement did exceptionally well after the American Revolution when more slaves gained their freedom. African Americans held a solid 20 percent presence from the late eighteenth century well into the nineteenth century.[48] As mentioned before, revivals appealed to Black people but also to the White seekers. The Awakening affected everyone equally. Many initially understood Methodism as a movement that opened the door to all people despite, gender, ethnicity, or class. "This new status produced a condition of liminality, a threshold of new experience that Methodists shared with one another."[49] Under Methodism, all Christians became brothers and sisters despite their background. They became one body, as Paul suggested in 1 Corinthians. Colonial America was driven by status, as was Corinth, and Methodism broke away from that mold initially. "The Methodist message was an egalitarian one, although Methodists were not completely able to live out this egalitarian ideology."[50] Methodism was deemed radical, and many were disconcerted by the message, especially in the South.[51]

45. Peter C. Murray, *Methodists and the Crucible of Race: 1930–1975* (Columbia: University of Missouri Press, 2004).
46. Murray, *Methodists and the Crucible of Race*, 42.
47. Ibid.
48. Ibid.
49. Ibid. 10.
50. Ibid.
51. Ibid.

Black people were not only drawn to the openness of Methodism but also to its opposition to slavery. The founder of the Methodist movement, John Wesley, spoke very candidly about his concerns for slavery and refused to consume anything produced out of slave labor. "Wesley wrote his anti-slavery tract in 1774 in which he asserted that, 'Liberty is the right of every human creature, as soon as he breathes the vital air and no human law can deprive him of that right.'"[52] In 1780, at a meeting in Baltimore, Methodist leaders agreed that slavery was "contrary to the laws of God, man, and nature, and hurtful to society, contrary to the dictates of conscience and pure religion."[53] About five years later, the first *Discipline* condemned slavery and prohibited members from owning slaves. If members had acquired slaves, they were given two years to free them.[54]

Black people were also drawn to the Methodist worship experience, which was rooted in "preaching, praise, and hymn singing." The worship experience was upbeat, had feeling, and it offered Black people biblical knowledge that had previously been denied to them. They were encouraged to delve deeper in their faith. Conversion was no longer the end-all for Black Christians. They desired to know and experience God on a deeper, emotional level expressed inwardly and outwardly.[55]

In the 1830s, race began to cause divisions in The Methodist Episcopal Church in addition to divisions over church polity.[56] The church's retreat from their antislavery position marked the beginning of a social shift that would trouble the church for

52. Murray, *Methodists and the Crucible of Race*, 11.
53. Ibid.
54. Ibid.
55. Murray, *Methodists and the Crucible of Race*, 12.
56. Murray, *Methodists and the Crucible of Race*, 13.

decades. Just six months after the first *Discipline* was written in 1785, the church suspended its rules against slavery.[57] The divisions on slavery led to the development of two separate issues of the *Discipline*, whereas the Southern version failed to mention slavery entirely.[58] Over time, Methodists' values were compromised as they sought to gain more membership and establish more congregations in the South.[59] Their growing leniency harmed the church's relationship with its Black members. Classes had become segregated, and conflicts arose between Black and White members over equality.[60] "At St. George Methodist Church in 1792, angry ushers who wanted Black members to pray last, after Whites were finished, dragged leaders Richard Allen and Absalom Jones to their feet while at the altar."[61] They were also denied communion until all of the White members had received the sacrament. The most significant issue, however, for Black Methodists concerned their rights to be leaders in the church. Several Black ministers, including Richard Allen, were ordained only as deacons. This was problematic because deacons were not permitted to administer the sacraments of baptism and communion, nor were they allowed to officiate at weddings.[62]

Richard Allen eventually left St. George's, established the Free African Society with Absalom Jones, and later established Bethel Methodist Church.[63] White paternalism plagued the Black church, including Allen's. White presiding elders were

57. Murray, *Methodists and the Crucible of Race*, 13.
58. Ibid., 13.
59. Ibid.
60. Murray, *Methodists and the Crucible of Race*, 14.
61. Ibid.
62. Ibid.
63. Ibid.

required for all Black congregations because Black ministers were not permitted to be ordained as elders.[64] At one point, St. George's, which had ties to New Bethel, attempted to appoint a new preacher "to New Bethel," and their presiding elder, James Smith, was contested in court on this issue.[65] The court ruled in Allen's favor and ordered that St. George's no longer had any authority over New Bethel.[66] "This was a blow to White paternal control and monopoly of church power; Bethel had grown to become one of the largest Methodist congregations in America."[67] It's plausible The Methodist Church could have avoided the major schism between Black and White members if it had been willing to simply ordain Black ministers as elders and accept them as members of annual conferences.[68] Despite their efforts, the Methodists could not escape the social norms of America. "White American society assumed its supremacy over African Americans, slave or free, and the liminal enthusiasm of Methodists became less common and racial prejudice more prevalent."[69]

The schism between Black and White Methodists didn't end the tensions regarding race. Slavery remained an issue for the church. The General Conference of 1844 supported the Baltimore Conference's decision to deny ordination for a candidate who owned a slave, but the breaking point concerned the status of Bishop James O Andrew, who inherited a slave through his wife.[70] General Conference leadership asked the bishop to

---

64. Murray, *Methodists and the Crucible of Race*, 15.
65. Ibid.
66. Ibid.
67. Ibid.
68. Ibid.
69. Ibid.
70. Murray, *Methodists and the Crucible of Race*, 17.

step down, and the Southern Methodists were infuriated by this. "Southern Methodists found this unacceptable, and they announced their intent to form a new church, one cleansed of antislavery sentiment."[71] After the North and the South split, they each maintained African American membership but continued to "supervise" their congregations. Even after Black congregations were formed, White Christians did their best to exercise their control. It's interesting to note that White Christians felt the need to dictate to Black Christians how they should be doing church after they virtually drove them out of their churches. Though Black Christians found more autonomy in forming their churches, inequality was still an issue in their places of worship. It should also be noted that both the Northern and Southern churches proceeded to supervise the Black congregations. This was not only a Southern dynamic.

The Southern Methodist Church sought to alter the message of Christianity to enforce its pro-slavery agenda.

Many Southern slaveholders allowed The Methodist Episcopal Church, South, to organize congregations among their slaves so that their slaves might internalize values of loyalty and honesty. Masters saw Christianity as a means of extending their authority and making their slaves more agreeable.[72]

Finally, in 1864, the Northern church approved the ordination of African American ministers as elders.[73] This was a victory for Black Methodists, but they still faced a long journey ahead. After the Civil War, Black Methodists continued to fight tooth and nail to gain equality by pushing for the election of Black

---

71.   Murray, *Methodists and the Crucible of Race*, 17.
72.   Ibid.
73.   Murray, *Methodists and the Crucible of Race*, 18.

bishops. The General Conference stated that Black elders would be eligible to be elected to the episcopacy, but Black bishops were never elected before 1920.[74] In fact, "19th century efforts to elect an African American bishop reached their zenith in 1896, when Dr. John Wesley Bowen led all voting on the first ballot for the episcopacy."[75] Despite this fact, he was not elected, and Black Methodists in the Northern church were terribly disappointed.[76]

Segregation

The formation of the Central Jurisdiction was another blow to the strained relationship between Black and White Methodists. The Methodist Episcopal Churches of the North and South, along with The Methodist Protestant Church, merged to become The Methodist Church in 1939. "Equal to five regional jurisdictional conferences, the Central Jurisdiction could elect its own bishops and had representation on national church boards and agencies."[77] Black Methodist churches, despite their geographical locations, were placed in one jurisdiction in order to limit their authority within the denomination and to cultivate a "separate but equal" structure.[78] The formation of the Central Jurisdiction served to placate those who were disinterested in being a part of an interracial church. At the root of The Methodist Episcopal Church's separation, years prior, was the contention regarding slavery. Despite the fact that this move was not favored by all, it accomplished White Methodists' goal of reunification. In effect,

74. Murray, Methodists and the Crucible of Race, 22.
75. Murray, Methodists and the Crucible of Race, 23.
76. Ibid., 23.
77. Murray, Methodists and the Crucible of Race, 3.
78. Ibid.

their compromise deepened the wound concerning race relations in the church. The efforts to end the Central Jurisdiction were controversial and there were differences in opinion regarding the best approach. The Methodist Church never elected to end the Central Jurisdiction officially. The jurisdiction was not included in the new United Methodist denomination of 1968 due greatly to The Evangelical United Brethren's refusal to merge under the race-based structure.

It would appear the church in many places still maintains the "separate but equal" mindset. When recalling this history, it's easy to understand why. We've never dealt with our racist past. Over the years, blanket statements have been made on the connectional level. Apologies have been expressed for the formation of the Central Jurisdiction but the efforts taken to atone for the church's complicity in racism minimally affect the local church. The local church is where one may experience the separation most significantly. The structure of the Methodist church may have changed in 1968, but it did little to change the mindset of many who believed Black and White people should not worship together. It did little to eradicate White paternalism. It did little to empower more White Christians to speak out against racial injustice. Black Methodists who were a part of the Central Jurisdiction articulated very clearly that more work should be done to eradicate racism than to simply undo a racist structure.

Years ago, upon learning more about this history, I asked my former seminary professor, Bishop Woodie White, "Why would Black people remain in an institution that was so terribly unkind to them?" He explained to me that many felt they had more to lose by walking away. They invested in a number of churches and schools across the country that were nurturing to their communities. They simply could not walk away from all that they'd built and fought for. I'm amazed and empowered by their strength and resilience. Perhaps at the root of their strength was their faith in Jesus. Perhaps they believed that Jesus is bigger than racism and discrimination. Perhaps their faith in Jesus's power and presence in their lives is what kept them going. Perhaps they didn't need to feel the acceptance and validation of those who were oppressing them because Jesus had welcomed each of them with open arms and it was his love that validated them. His life and teachings exemplify the true nature of seeing the other, loving the other, and speaking on behalf of the other. These are the reasons why I chose to walk with Jesus. I've spent my life navigating this world as a Black woman, and when I met Jesus, I finally felt seen, loved, and spoken for.

Today's church is a by-product of our history. Though many are not aware of our history, we are indeed a part of it. This simply can't be what John Wesley intended for Methodism. As previously mentioned, Methodism appealed to Black people because of the inclusive message that was presented to them. John Wesley spoke candidly about his disapproval of American slavery and asserted in "Thoughts on Slavery" that all people should be honored with dignity. We tend to forget that social justice was at the core of the early Methodist movement. The concept of loving the neighbor became practical and social. Loving the neighbor meant seeing the neighbor, valuing the neighbor, and standing for the neighbor when necessary. The Methodism I grew to love sought to serve the world and not itself. It didn't compromise values in order to conform to social norms.

Black Christians, battered by the effects of racism in the church, nurtured their own churches and established their own traditions. The Black church became a retreat from the troubles of the world, a place of solace for Black Christians. In having conversations on race and the possibility of churches becoming more diverse, it has become clear to me that many Black Christians tend to be more hesitant than Whites. History tells us that Black Christians were pushed away by their White counterparts. Once we worshipped together. Once we attempted to be the body of Christ that the Apostle Paul celebrates in 1 Corinthians 12:12-13: "Christ is just like the human body—a body is a unit and has many parts; and all the parts of the body are one body, even though there are many. We were all baptized by one Spirit into one body, whether Jew or Greek, or slave or free, and we all were given one Spirit to drink." Many Black Christians ask the question, What is it worth now when we've been down that painful road before?

Reconciliation

I'm fighting for reconciliation because it's clear the wounds of the past are still present whether we seek to acknowledge them or not. I'm currently serving a cross-racial appointment in the Memphis Conference of The UMC and have led a number of studies on race with my congregation and neighboring churches. Many were shocked to learn of our past and had been Methodists for decades. They were raised in racially homogenous churches, as I was, and assumed the structure was normal. Several have shared their interest in being a part of a worship experience that is more diverse, but this isn't achievable for any church until racial reconciliation takes place. The journey toward reconciliation begins with the church's willingness to face our past and stand in the truth of who we call ourselves to be. Conversations must take place and friendships must be fostered across racial lines. I've found, in working toward reconciliation, that the same core people will always show up to do the work. In order for the church to truly overcome our challenges involving race, this must be a collective effort among our local churches. The entire church must be on board. It was my father's friendship with a White pastor down the road that opened my eyes to the dynamics of race that had surrounded me my entire life, but this partnership would not have been successful if both congregations had not chosen to open their hearts to one another. God is always calling us to challenge ourselves and the structures that serve us more than others.

Chapter Six

I'M BLACK. I'M PASTOR OF A WHITE METHODIST CHURCH.

Justin Coleman

Senior Pastor, University United Methodist Church,
Chapel Hill, North Carolina

Origin Story: Living above Flight

I love a good origin story. If you're a fan of literature, comic books, or mythology, then you know that origin stories matter. Origin stories also matter in biblical literature for God's people. My origin story is about growing up in a predominantly White community in north Houston, because it shaped the ministry I'm a part of today.

Jaco Hamman, who teaches at Vanderbilt Divinity School, explains to students that we as Christians (and certainly as theologians and pastors) are taught by multiple seminaries. A seminary teaches us about God and how to understand and interpret the Christian faith and how to interact with and understand the people of God. The first seminary is that of the home, the second seminary is that of the community (including schools and other community organizations), the third seminary is the church, the fourth seminary is higher education, and the fifth seminary is graduate education (schools of divinity and theology). In each place we learn something about how we are to understand God and the people of God. We learn how to interact with the image of God within each other, or we learn how to resist the image of God and each other.

My children have grown up with images of President Barack and First Lady Michelle Obama on the national and international stage. They've grown up with superheroes like the Black Panther on the big screen. As a child, I only dreamed of such images. I had depictions of largely White males who would have you believe that they were supermen. But in my imagination, Superman could indeed be Black. After all, he lived among those who were different from him, who didn't always accept him, and he had powers they could not always recognize. Sure, he could fit in if he wanted to, but when it was time for him to stand up in the defense of the vulnerable, he was formidable. This kind of formidability beyond conformity is what I have so often seen lived out in Black bodies and through Blackness.

Superman primarily had Jonathan and Martha Kent to take care of him, but I was glad to have the equivalent of Jor-El and Lara to take care of me. My parents, Austin and Elaine Coleman, insisted that we dressed well according to the conventions of the community that we lived in, that we spoke with excellent diction and grammar and never used slang; and that we did our very best in school. While growing up, there was never a White standard. Our parents were the standard that we had to live up to. If we missed the mark somehow, our parents were the ones to which we would give account. There was something very powerful about Blackness, not Whiteness, the standard we had to live up to. I was also blessed by some White Jonathans and Marthas along the way. The "Kents" were teachers, Sunday school teachers, and clergy who supported and encouraged me along the way. My fifth-grade teacher, Mr. Laich, was one such person. Mr. Laich took it upon himself one day while mostly students and teachers were gathered near to tell me that he didn't have a son, but if he did he would want his son to be just like me. At the time I didn't recognize the significance of his statement. As one of the beloved and well-respected teachers in the school, he was looking at a mostly all-White audience and saying to them that this Black kid had in some way excelled. He'd occasionally ask me if I'd seen the latest episode of "A Different World," a show that I'd told the class that my family watched, and he'd talk about the colleges that I might go to when I was older. I appreciate all the folks like him who knew the importance of encouraging a Black student in an almost all-White school.

The suburban neighborhood I grew up in was born out of White flight from the inner city of Houston. Our family was one of the first families to integrate our neighborhood, and so my parents were always very concerned that we be safe in the midst of this integration. My father had grown up in Mississippi, and his family had seen firsthand the results of an angry White population that surrounded them. My grandmother, my father, and my uncle were run out of town when my father was young, under threat of the potential lynching of my uncle. My mother and father had a clear sense that unless we were all watchful and vigilant that things can go sideways easily. As parents, they were protectors of their children, they taught us how to watch and be watchful, to be mindful of our situation and the conditions around us. My parents did all this, however, in a way that never made us afraid of our environment. Mom and Dad blocked for us and protected us in ways that we could not even see at the time. They were regularly in parent-teacher conferences and in principals' offices, not because their children had committed some kind of offense but because my parents considered that the practices in the educational systems were offensive to their children. My parents regularly reminded me of that scene from the *Lord of the Rings* trilogy when Gandalf enters the hall of Theodin. Those accompanying him block for him to keep all aggressors away so that Gandalf could approach Theodin to exorcise this spirit that had taken him captive. My parents wanted their children to be able to enter into any hall anywhere with boldness and to be who we were called to be and be able to do what we were called to do, so they blocked for us and made sure to the best of their ability that no harm came to us. My parents also taught us how to navigate the Whiteness around us wisely, so that we could take care of ourselves. My parents weren't perfect, but they loved us and worked hard to make sure that we knew we were Black, beautiful, intelligent, and that we need not think that anyone was superior. My parents reminded us that we, like everyone else, were created just "lower than angels" (Heb 2:7).

If you are Black and born in the United States of America, you are born into what W. E. B. Du Bois called "double consciousness." In his 1903 book, *The Souls of Black Folk*, Du Bois talks about double consciousness as "this sense of always looking at oneself through the eyes of others." One consciousness is that of your African American heritage and the other is a conscious born out of White supremacy. Black British author and scholar Paul Gilroy describes this consciousness in his groundbreaking work, *The Black Atlantic*. Gilroy encourages occupying the space between the dialectics of double consciousness, and in so doing a single identity emerges from this double consciousness. The single identity Gilroy speaks of is a resistance to the forces of White supremacy because this identity doesn't allow Whiteness to dominate. Gilroy speaks of a transcendent Black identity, one that is African, American, Caribbean, and British all at once. I appreciate Gilroy's attempt to say that Blackness is more that what it is conceived of through the eyes of others and I always felt that growing up. Blackness is a superpower—it is a social and political skill born out of the challenge of double consciousness.

While I was still in my north Houston equivalent of Smallville, and before a stronger identity was formed in me, I felt caught in between worlds. I was too Black to fit in well with the White folks. And I was around too many White folks to fit in well with all the Black folks. It was not that there was some small space between the world and me; it was as if there was space between worlds (plural) and me. So I sought to unite the worlds and develop space where I could be authentically me. This was also a space into which I could invite others, where kinship could be created and where I could help others move to some degree beyond more rigid racial boundaries we had created for ourselves. Essentially I learned to develop a multicultural, multiracial, and multinational group of friends. Through these friendships and an examination of the multinational/multilingual church that was birthed at Pentecost, I also began to see a vision for what the church could be.

Black and Methodist

I started my formal seminary journey at Perkins School of Theology in Dallas, Texas. I was from Texas and most United

Methodist ministers I'd known had gone to Perkins School of Theology. People had good things to say about Perkins and its formation, but for the most part people said if you want to learn how to preach well then you must learn from Zan Holmes. This was always said in the way that Obi-Wan told Luke to go to the Dagobah system to learn from Yoda. Black clergy told me to go to Pastor Holmes. White clergy told me to go to Pastor Holmes. Everybody said you have to go and learn from Zan Holmes. But Black clergy added something that was very important to me. Black clergy said go to Perkins, and Zan Holmes will teach you how to be Black and Methodist. When you are an African American clergy member, you send a student to a church as much as you send them to a seminary. Zan Holmes was pastor of St. Luke "Community" United Methodist Church. I was being sent to that church as much as I was being sent to Perkins seminary. It was at St. Luke that I would learn what it meant to be Black and Methodist.

I'd grown up going to a Black Baptist church in town, and then I'd become Methodist as a youth by joining a predominantly White United Methodist church just outside our neighborhood that was pastored by the father of one of my good friends. In Dallas, I would discover a different kind of Methodist than I'd seen. St. Luke "Community" UMC had excellent worship services that held fidelity to the general flow of United Methodist liturgy as I had known it in the largely White UMC that I grew up in, but it had all the life and energy of worship in the Black tradition: excellent preaching, excellent choirs, and a fully embodied experience of praise. This church was the Black embodiment of Psalm 150, and I loved it. I loved every worship service that I went to. I loved every hour of every worship service that I went to. I've never seen a preacher knock the ball out of the park so consistently as Zan Wesley Holmes, Jr. I didn't grow up learning how to whoop like so many African American preachers that I had known. The Black church that we went to when I was younger was Wheeler Avenue Baptist Church, pastored by William A. Lawson. Rev. Lawson preached more along the lines of a Gardner C. Taylor or Martin Luther King Jr. His sermonic style was focused more on soaring prose and poetic imagery with a compelling song-like tone in the rise and fall of his voice, similar to what you might hear in King and Taylor, but like King and Taylor, he didn't whoop and holler. So that was Black preaching for me, which when coupled with my time in White churches meant that I never developed a whoop. If I developed any ability to simulate a good hallelujah shout, it came from Pastor Holmes, who is thoughtful, eloquent, socially engaged, exegetically sophisticated, and can holler with the best of them.

Pastor Holmes shared a story in a sermon near the time he was retiring. At one point before he came to St. Luke, he was a district superintendent and inside his district was First United Methodist Church, Dallas. First United Methodist Church was to be receiving a new pastor, and Zan Holmes was already a celebrated pastor and preacher in the conference. He was also concluding his time as district superintendent and thought that he could be the first African American preacher to become the senior pastor of First United Methodist Church. When the time came for appointments there'd been conversation with the staff-parish relations committee at the church and others and the prospects looked promising. One evening, all parties were gathered in a room together at First UMC with the bishop, staff-parish relations committee, and Pastor Holmes. In that meeting the bishop said that the day may come when Zan Holmes could be pastor of First United Methodist Church in Dallas, Texas, but that the time had not come. Pastor Holmes was crestfallen. This was the mid-1970s, and Methodism was not yet ready. After this disappointment, Pastor Holmes went to serve at a small church named St. Luke "Community" UMC. The United Methodist Church was not ready for this kind of highly visible cross-racial appointment to what it would consider one of its big White flagship churches. St. Luke "Community" United Methodist Church became a leading megachurch in many ways in the midst of the North Texas Annual Conference and our denomination. St. Luke's UMC was right where God wanted Zan Holmes. I also wonder what ministry First United Methodist Church lost out on because they could not receive a Black senior pastor.

Fifty years later, it's still considered a rarity for one of the big White flagship United Methodist churches in any annual conference to have an African American senior pastor. My current appointment is at one of the larger White churches in the annual conference I'm a part of, and when I arrived, I received messages from all around the country congratulating me for breaking a glass ceiling here. It pains me that we are still receiving calls like this in this part of the twenty-first century, but we know from the trauma of our society that we still have a very long way to go related to race relations outside and sadly inside the church.

Years ago I served as an associate pastor in the church I'm currently serving as senior pastor. Zan Holmes came to baptize our eldest son, who is named after him. Zan had such a great time at our church and said to me, "This church really loves you and they seem to be ready to receive your ministry." He reminded me of the story of his conversation with First United Methodist

Church in Dallas, and he said, "When there's a church that can accept and celebrate your ministry, you should try to stay there for a long time." I was an associate at University United Methodist Church, Chapel Hill, for only three years, but when, after a decade, the church asked me to come back as senior pastor, I called Zan Holmes and he was very happy that they had done so. For me, coming back to University United Methodist Church was coming back to a church in a community to which I felt called in this season, and that I felt had the capacity to have conversations about race and anti-racism. I also felt I could offer leadership in the Chapel Hill community. In other ways, this appointment also felt like a small vindication of everyone like Zan Holmes who has been told you can't serve this big White Methodist church because you are Black.

Breaking Down, Translating, and Building Up

I've long felt a calling to help congregations move toward a wider racial vision—specifically, helping White churches move toward a larger racial vision and working to create multiracial congregations. I see this work as honoring the work of Black United Methodists who decided to remain in The United Methodist Church after the creation of the all-Black Central Jurisdiction, which existed from 1939 through 1968. The decision on the part of some Black Methodists to remain in the Central Jurisdiction, while others who were incensed by its creation left, was in part an act of resistance. This was a decision to sit in this denomination until change happened. Remaining resisted the impulse of the White church to say that the races must be kept separated, therefore separate systems and separate churches must be created to segregate races. These brave Black United Methodists resisted the impulses that led to the creation of the Black Methodist denominations in years past. As long as we perpetuate and allow a separate but equal notion in our churches, we will continue to teach by our practice that United Methodists worship a God who condones segregation. Those who chose to leave The United Methodist Church did so for good reasons. We have needed, and indeed need today, spaces where African Americans can come together for community, support, and the celebration of culture. These distinctly African American spaces are psychologically healthy and often necessary in a country that continues to demonstrate to Black people that it believes our lives matter less than other lives. I believe that we need both psychologically healthy spaces and spaces of resistance.

I feel called to spaces of resistance, and I find that I have to work harder and harder each passing year to make sure that these places of resistance are psychologically healthy for my family. We live in a town that is very progressive in its self-identity and in the speech acts that it performs to support that identity. Yet, in this progressive space we have felt the pain of racism more than we have in any other place we have lived. Everywhere we go around town, in front of many residences there are banners and signs saying Black Lives Matter. Yet in this very same town, we experience, in terms of public school achievement scores, the second-largest disparity and opportunity gap between Black and White students in the entire country. In the same town, the number of African Americans who can afford to live inside the town decreases precipitously and historically. African American communities continue to gentrify at a rapid rate. The university known to be the "people's university" here in our town struggles to recruit African American students. In so many ways my progressive town continues to demonstrate that thriving Black lives matter less. I think very carefully about the psychological effect that this space of resistance has on me and has on my family. This place is not a place of ease for us. It is a place of struggle, a place of resistance, a place of necessary resistance. This progressive place is, in the words of the late John Lewis, a place to "get in good trouble, necessary trouble."

Having grown up in spaces where I was in a clear minority, I learned what it means to translate back and forth between the Black and White communities. This effort can be exhausting. Zan Holmes once said that if you are going to be a bridge, you have to be strong, because it means you are going to get walked on. By this he did not say that people won't respect you and will walk all over you. Pastor Holmes was saying that if you are going to be a bridge, you must be willing to carry the weight, the fear, and sometimes the confused and frustrated navigation of people who are trying to move from one side to the other. People who are bridges sometimes face lack of understanding from people on both sides of the chasm they are seeking to bridge.

My work of breaking down walls has largely been breaking down walls of ignorance or lack of understanding between the White communities that I serve as a pastor and the Black community and other communities of color. This work is long-suffering work and doesn't happen overnight. It happens over years. There are multiple ways a person might go about breaking down walls. Some people go in with a sledgehammer or a wrecking ball and try to knock the wall down. My method tends to be more like Joshua at the battle of Jericho. Take the spiritual resources and authority that one has been given by God and circle that wall. Sing the songs of faith around that wall, carry the interpreted sacred text around that wall, pray and shout to God around that wall, and then watch it fall. Breaking down walls is a very spiritual activity for me. This is a spiritual act of resistance. We spiritually resist sin. We spiritually resist those things that divide people. Racism is a large and imposing wall, but God can break down any wall. The notion of race itself is a wall that was constructed. In the days before Westerners and Western Christians created the notion of race, we identified ourselves by the place we were from. This wall between races was intentionally built, and Western Christianity has played a large role in the construction—by spreading notions of white supremacy. This wall has been made strong and reinforced across generations in North America.

The reality, however, is that we've grown accustomed to these walls, and, if we're honest, so many of us like these walls. If walls are all you know, they are normal, they are safe. The destruction of these walls threatens us. Destruction of these racial walls threatens the ways that we have learned to be God's people. One place that is an example of a new world is Homeboy Industries in Los Angeles. Homeboy is one of the rare places where I observe enemies becoming friends in a way that resonates deeply with scripture. When I imagine Revelation 7:9-17 and the great crowd gathered around God's throne, I imagine the crowd being filled with the love and kinship that I've seen at Homeboy. All divisions melted away and the only things left are love and kinship in the family of God. Once we get over the dividing hostility that has become so normal, so safe for us, then we enter into the grand new territory of kinship in God's kingdom.

Confronting and Acknowledging

When entering a new appointment, it's important to take enough time to understand the place where the church is located. Some congregations have rich and well-documented histories, but some don't. Just as a congregation has a story, so does the place in which the congregation is rooted. In the United States of America, every location has a history of race. This history should be confronted and acknowledged if we are to begin the work of healing from the racial scars on every community. In every place, BIPOC (Black, Indigenous, and People of Color) have suffered displacement, terror, and other types of trauma. In some cases, this suffering happened inside congregations or has been promulgated by those who sat in the pews of the congregations we serve.

In the season after the killing of George Floyd, Breonna Taylor, and Ahmaud Arbery, many White people throughout the United States began to read books on how to be antiracist. The pandemic lockdown created a captive audience that witnessed the terrors and horrors inflicted upon Black lives in the United States with renewed empathy. So many people want to be able to claim that they are not racist, and indeed that they are antiracist. For White people to actually be antiracist, antiracism must become more of a practice than a state of being. Part of being a Black senior pastor serving a majority White congregation is to help remind the congregation that they must practice being antiracist. Members of the congregation must learn that antiracism is not a passive nod but an active habit.

I serve in a "cross-racial appointment." My colleague Donnie Jones says it saddens him when people say he's in a cross-racial appointment, yet all the other United Methodist clergy he knows are simply said to be in an appointment. He wondered aloud why we who are of another race than the majority of our congregation require a special designation for our appointments. Instead, I wish all United Methodist ministers thought of their appointments as antiracist appointments. Each of us by our ordination and by our calling as God's children ought to be actively resisting racism in our congregations and in our world, because we seek to resist evil, injustice, and oppression in whatever forms they present themselves as a part of our baptismal vows. Clergy should become antiracist at all levels of their church and society. For White clergy and parishioners, that work begins by acknowledging how racism manifests in the behaviors of individuals, systems, and places.

Kinship: A More Just and Inclusive Vision

Father Gregory Boyle of Homeboy Industries says, "No kinship, no justice. No kinship, no peace." An understanding of kinship in Christ is, I believe, the vision to which all Christian communities must move. Kinship requires dismantling of our understanding about the origins of race and building a new social construction.

Willie James Jennings said that race is created within a set of extremes. On the one extreme was Blackness and on the other was Whiteness. Blackness was said to be inferior and Whiteness was said to be superior. Every person from every country and society was placed in between these two poles. In this supremacist racial system, either people groups are moved toward Whiteness with its notions of superiority, or they are moved toward Blackness and are told they are inferior. In this system, you see the pursuit of

Whiteness emerge. People from countries that were not originally considered White, such as Germany, sought to achieve the status of Whiteness. People from parts of the Middle East sought to achieve the status of Whiteness. Latinx people sought to seek the status of Whiteness. People sought to pass as being White.

The social construction of Whiteness is anti-Trinitarian. The Triune God embodies unity, and humanity is created in God's image. This image of God is relational, it is diverse, and it is beautiful. This image of God is to be celebrated. The creation of races as a polarity between Blackness and Whiteness is counter to God's creation. The social construction of race is, therefore, anti-Christ. Anything that is against the witness of God in Christ Jesus is, by definition, anti-christ.

Pentecost and the Tower of Babel in Genesis remind us that God cares about diversity. God cares about the diversity of languages and cultures. God cares enough to allow persons of every country, every culture, and every language to hear the good news in their own language and be a part of God's family without the need to assimilate into any particular cultural norm. God creates a family with all this rich diversity. Pentecost is a reminder that we were already family in the first place as children of God. We are bound together by spiritual and temporal bonds of kinship that God created and called good.

Again, in Revelation 7:9-17, we see this great crowd. And no matter where we think we are headed in this world and no matter who we believe should be there with us, this vision that John of Patmos shared is where we are all headed. John saw us there and all of our rich and creative diversity, and we were all one. A kindred community is where we are all headed and our lives in this world as Christians should testify to this reality. In my ministry of resistance, I yearn to embody this vision. There are many hard days, but they will not be so forever.

> "These people have come out of great hardship. They have washed their robes and made them white in the Lamb's blood. This is the reason they are before God's throne. They worship him day and night in his temple, and the one seated on the throne will shelter them. . . . Because the Lamb who is in the midst of the throne will shepherd them. He will lead them to the springs of life-giving water, and God will wipe away every tear from their eyes." (Rev 7:14b, 17)

Chapter Seven

I'M BLACK. I STUTTER.
I TEACH IN A WHITE CHURCH.

Jevon A. Caldwell-Gross

Teaching Pastor, St. Luke's United Methodist Church, Indianapolis, Indiana

The Power of Voice

My voice has always been a source of insecurity. I stutter. I
wish I didn't, but I do. If you listen long enough, it will eventually
unveil itself. It could happen at the introduction of my name, a
reading of scripture, or while explaining something to one of my
three children. Sometimes I daydream about how different life
would be, how confident and outgoing I would appear, if God
would miraculously remove this thorn from my side. I envy people who can stand before a room and speak without difficulty. I
admire the person who moves seamlessly through a crowd with
witty jokes and perfectly timed comebacks. I marvel at the skill of
being able to say exactly what one wishes without obstacles, hic-
cups, or syllabus repetitions. I have conceded that the answer to
that prayer may never come, so I've learned how to live with this
reality. My insecurities have only heightened my understanding of
how essential one's voice can be.

The Bible affirms the power of voice. As Genesis begins, the world is introduced to a God that stares out into an abyss of emptiness and says, "Let there be. . . ." The first miracle sets creation into motion. Of all options available for an omnipotent God, the chosen instrument was the voice. In the second creation story, Genesis 2, God creates through touch and direct connection to the creation. In this narrative, we see God's theological commitment to using the powerful instrument of voice in the story of creation and redemption. Its power is displayed as a creative, life-giving force that has transforming qualities. Contextually, mere words would seem so inconsequential and even ineffective against the realities of the surrounding contexts.

In these first few verses, quite the contrary is true. Unafraid and unintimidated by the infinite depths of darkness, this voice courageously speaks. This same voice was not inhibited by precedence or complexity but continued to offer verbal commands prompting existence. The voice had the audacity to call out that which was not in existence: light, the atmosphere, animals, humanity in existence and even rest. God spoke life into existence. This voice spoke order into chaos. It was intentional. It was relentless. It could have easily acquiesced and surrendered to the present context or abated due to the void, but it persisted. It pushed through every obstacle. Even the darkness could not silence it. This was a voice with unprecedented power. Sometimes I wonder what it would sound like if God stuttered creation into existence.

As God's narrative unfolds, so does God's voice. What happened in Genesis foreshadows the possibilities of such a divine instrument that would eventually become real in the lives of everyday people. As we move to the life and ministry of Jesus Christ, this same voice with the power to create and transform the world stays true to itself. Several years, chapters, and generations beyond the transformative power of this prior voice, we find the same voice is now coming from the mouth of a carpenter in the Middle East. This power wasn't the result of a prestigious title bestowed upon him by a religious or civic institution. It was not the consequence of spending years being associated with the most well-known minds or religious leaders. A different kind of power was connected with this voice. As we watch this narrative unfold, we find Genesis 1 lived out in very tangible ways.

The context has dramatically changed, but the results are no less impactful. When Jesus starts his earthly ministry, this voice shows a mirrored responsibility and ability to bring light into darkness. Again, this voice is both intentional and persistent. Walking by a familiar location for fishermen in the community, this voice would call these ordinary fishermen to be and become something they had never envisioned for themselves. Unfazed and unaffected by societal expectations, he courageously calls them to something more. From the same voice of the carpenter, he was unafraid to command a woman who had been bent over for eighteen years to stand up straight. He had the audacity to say to a man who sat by a pool for decades, "Pick up your mat and walk" (John 55:11). Not even the religious leaders could refute this voice. His words were powerful enough to throw out the legions that possessed a man. Even as his close friend Lazarus lay dead in the grave displaying signs and smell of apparent death, Jesus could speak to the emptiness in the tomb and command Lazarus's dead body to come out at once. It wasn't just what Jesus did that threatened the religious leaders, but it was what he said. It was the power of his voice that they could not comprehend. His voice could heal bodies.

His voice could speak to impossible situations. His voice could forgive people of their sins. Even the storms had to obey his voice. They could not explain the origin of his power, they only knew that when he spoke people came alive and the laws of nature seemed to make exceptions.

Rest assured, this display of power was not without its own obstacles or temptations. The willingness for this voice to persist was nothing short of a miracle. There were several competing voices in Jesus's community. He had to contend with the looming voices of the Roman political leaders. There were the threats from religious leaders. But this creative, powerful, and transformative instrument persisted. It didn't shrink at the threat of Roman rule or the low expectations of familiar faces. It didn't acquiesce to the religious laws that governed human connections. It didn't even bend or break when standing against the laws of nature and utter impossibility. No situation was dark enough, no situation bleak enough, no threat dangerous enough to suppress its power.

Many of us are not so fortunate. If the power of voice has always been present, so too will be the temptation of suppression. For several years I allowed my own insecurities to silence my voice. I became adept at acquiescing to the circumstances around me. But we all run the risk of having our voices silenced. There are moments when its seems like our mere words are no match for the current conditions of our lives or the world in which we live. Too often, we've surveyed the feelings of those around us, we've counted the cost, we've peered into the darkness, and the temptation to muzzle our own voices seemed like the only option. We've all been there; until we find our voices.

Finding My Voice

While I spent years perfecting ways to hide my voice and mask my imperfections, the Black Church was influential in helping me find the significance through the stutter. It gave me the space to find what I so desperately wanted to hide. Every voice needs a space free from suppression.

I found this in my home church in Detroit. My religious upbringing was formed through the African Methodist Episcopal Zion Church. This was my first introduction into a Methodist faith expression. The church of my youth introduced me to a God that heard the cry of the needy and delivered people from Egyptian slavery. This God seemed to be concerned about the daily affairs of everyone sitting in the pew. Hopeful refrains, such as "His Eye Is on the Sparrow" or "I Want Jesus to Walk with Me," were helpful reminders of a personal and compassionate God. I heard this hope in the early Christian hymn in Philippians 2:6-11, at the sound of his voice every knee must bow and every tongue shall confess that Jesus Christ is Lord. This was not a large congregation or the most socially responsive, but there never seemed to be a reticence to address the daily concerns of the people who looked like me. This faith expression readily included the names and accomplishments of Black faith leaders like James Varick, Richard Allen, and Absalom Jones. I willingly chose to be a part of this faith tradition.

I was not aware of it at the time, but these experiences were not only shaping my faith but were also molding and maturing my voice. As a freshman in college, I gave my first sermon before the congregation, and they affirmed my call to preach. This was quite the affirmation for someone with my insecurity. It gave my voice a space. This journey took on new meaning when I was given an opportunity to be a pastor within The United Methodist Church. Like many others, I was affirmed that my gifts fit a growing need within our conference as the number of Black clergy was dwindling. While I no longer heard about the dynamic Black faith leaders in my own Methodist upbringing, the opportunity was critical for my own voice. For the next eight years, I would pastor two predominantly Black congregations within The United Methodist Church.

During one of the darkest moments of our nation's recent history, I found my voice. Dylann Roof walked into Emmanuel AME Church in Charleston, South Carolina, and killed nine African Americans. I recall looking at the response from my colleagues and at my inner circle on social media, and the message was quite clear. If you weren't addressing this in your congregation, then your members should find another church. The social media community was quite clear that this was a necessary time for Black voices to speak to the very real darkness spreading across our nation. But voices have power. It was the clearest moment that I felt the call that was expressed in Genesis 1. I had to abandon my scheduled train of thought for that particular Sunday and address what seemed to be the same darkness and impossibility found within the first few pages of the Bible. But this darkness had a name and a history, which one could track and measure. This darkness had too long festered in the silence of faith traditions. Whatever insecurities were present no longer mattered. I abandoned my entire sermon. In my feeble attempts, I tried to highlight the very realities that many of us faced on our daily basis and yet tried to give life and hope. I titled the sermon that following Sunday "When Holy Ground Becomes the Battle Ground."

As the news swept across the media and social media platforms, one could feel the hurt and fear in the Black community. While the emotions were present, so also were the expectations of repression. It's not written in a company memo, but it's what our nation requires of Black voices. What often goes unsaid regarding those affected by these and other traumatic events is the unspoken expectation that we are expected to walk into our jobs and into public spaces calm and composed. We are to carry on with business as usual. While there are such differing opinions on rioting and the correct ways to respond to injustice, the amount of restraint that is required to not live out the rage and years of repression is rarely mentioned. No one discusses the number of instances where many from the Black community have been expected to cry silently in private spaces and then walk into work the very next day unaffected.

When President Trump was elected, genuine fear erupted within many vulnerable communities. Our worst nightmares had become a reality: at its core, a large majority of our nation didn't hold race and issues of justice as a primary concern. His comments and connections didn't go unnoticed. While millions celebrated his rise to the presidency, it struck a chord of fear and instability for many others. Again, my voice mattered. The Sunday after the votes were counted, I knew that I had to stand before a congregation and give them assurance of God's Providence and to remind them that God still cared. This wasn't a matter of political discourse, but it was a very real reminder that his election exposed a side of America that people knew existed but didn't want to acknowledge. Out from the shadows, hatred and division became a dominant narrative that we are still experiencing today. As I write these words I'm seeing notifications about a federal ban regarding the use of antiracist training materials within federal agencies and in school curricula.

For many like myself, the church became one of a few places that gave us the space to grieve unapologetically and voice our fears unashamedly. It was here where I realized that my young, Black, stuttering voice mattered. I would gladly choose to give my voice to this journey Sunday after Sunday. While some communities may associate justice with an extracurricular biblical activity, in these moments of repression and denial, Black voices are essential for helping people cope with the traumatic possibility that people who look like me can be killed, or someone I know can die at the hands of police or street vigilantes. In my own congregation, I heard the fear of parents about their sons, and wives about their husbands each time these men got in the car. Rather than silence, we could wear hooded sweatshirts for a Sunday to show a concerted effort and to bring attention to the atrocities of the death of young and gifted Trayvon Martin. We could affirm that Black lives mattered without apology or excuse.

The Death of Black Voices

Declining numbers is one of the reasons why it's hard being Black and Methodist. This culture is quickly dying. While many of our major cities are experiencing increased levels of diversity and growth, many ethnic churches are closing or have declined to the point of irrelevancy. My experience might shed some light.

My first appointment in The United Methodist Church was to a small declining Black church located in southern New Jersey. My second appointment was larger in size, but it was suffering the same kind of decline. Not a single day passes that I'm not grateful for the experience and the relationships formed in both of these congregations. I would eventually learn that my experience was the norm. Many of our Black churches in or around our urban cities were in steep decline. However, my very first Sunday in that first congregation revealed a tension between Black voices in predominantly White denominations. Before I was able to find my voice, I had to fight against another.

As I sat through the service of my first Sunday as a solo pastor, I felt like an outsider—not in relationships but in culture. I didn't recognize the songs or the tunes. For several weeks, we repeated the assigned responsive liturgy, we sang the selected hymns, and we then retreated to our respective homes. This liturgy was not in a voice I recognized.

I could not articulate the narrative that was unfolding until one visitor's expectations allowed me to articulate the source of this tension. As a town bustling with tourists in the summer, it was common for new faces to visit as the weather warmed. One Sunday, a Caucasian woman arrived before service and waited patiently. In order to set an example of hospitality, I introduced myself, and she admitted this was not her first time in the congregation. She shared that she was an out-of-town guest, but wanted to find a Black church in the area because she loved gospel music and admired the worship experience of the Black churches she had previously attended. That's when the veil was lifted and I could finally articulate the tension I felt within my own congregation. I didn't admit this to her, but I knew that her expectations were not going to be met.

Black expressions of faith or Methodism aren't all the same. They will vary with demographics, region, and size of the congregation. But regardless of where it's located, the liturgy and nurture should reflect the voices and unique experience of that community. There was an unspoken fear and expectation in this small congregation that we had to emulate a voice that was not authentically our own in order to meet the standards of being Methodist. The value and lens by which we perceived worship was a White cultural lens. We tried so hard to fit into a narrow view of Methodism that we no longer shared a relevant connection with the community we were called to serve. We were willing to sacrifice our own voices in order to be good "Methodists."

The church couldn't grow until I came to accept this hard reality: no one in that community cared about John Wesley, his brother, playing the correct tune as it was written in the hymnal, or any of our creeds. That's hard for some to hear. But in this moment of reality, I could articulate the inherit struggle between being Black and being United Methodist. This was not a space that started with our voices or our experiences. Being Methodist meant that one had to leave an aspect of one's self and unique cultural experiences behind.

I would learn that this tension is not unique to this first appointment. I was appointed pastor to another congregation in Northern New Jersey after four years. After the experiences of my previous congregation, I asked to see the bulletin before my first Sunday. While browsing the twenty-one-page document, I recognized its voice. The words of my predecessor haunt me to this day. While well intentioned with undeniable wisdom and a heart of gold, he admitted that the purpose of the dramatic shift was to help the congregation become more Methodist. Ironically, the first Black church in this quaint city showed very few signs of its cultural and historical experience through its own worship. In an attempt to become more Methodist, that unique voice had been completely erased. While both of these congregations grew, it was not due to a long list of great ideas but a willingness by members to look deeply into their own communities and start the conversation in a voice that they and their communities recognized.

But that's how systematic racism flourishes. White cultural norms become the standard by which people along the margins view ourselves and our experiences. Success and acceptability become an act of ventriloquism and not the harmony of our own unique and collective voices. We must become experts and knowledgeable about the lives, customs, and thoughts of an entire movement that rarely included persons from our experience. After nearly eleven years in The UMC, I have yet to hear the names of faith leaders such as James Varick and Absalom Jones. I fear that as Black Methodist churches attempt to assimilate with a White European culture, the worship spaces for grief in an oppressed Black culture, which truly values our voice, are quickly dying.

Black Voices in White Spaces

I didn't know at time that serving these Black churches would be a personal lesson in suppression. After serving as the pastor in two predominantly Black United Methodist congregations, my wife and I received an offer to join the staff at one of the largest United Methodist churches located in the Midwest. I willingly chose to offer my voice to a predominantly White congregation. We made the commitment to ourselves that we would bring our authentic voices to this new space.

I admit that no one plans to have their voices silenced. No one methodically charts their own suppression; but it happens. For years, I worried that my stuttering would be the cause of my silence, but I was proved wrong. For the previous eight years, I thought I was successful in helping other congregations reclaim their own voices, but I didn't know my voice would suffer the same fate. Without realizing how or why, I just knew that one day it was gone.

I previously found my voice as a light in the darkness, but a similar situation would reveal the opposite. After Ahmaud Arbery's senseless death, I was scheduled to go "live" on Facebook. This had become a weekly routine during the COVID-19 pandemic. I vacillated about whether I should address the topic. If I did, what would I say? Was this even my role as an associate pastor? How could I tell the truth in front of this White audience without offending them? I followed protocol by informing the senior pastor of my preferred topic and theological direction. I decided that I couldn't with a good conscience speak in front of any audience (even if it's through a computer screen) and not address what our nation couldn't ignore. I made sure I was selective with my words. I stayed clear of certain controversial words and names. This was a far cry from the voice that I remembered. Where did it go? Many Black voices have died and been silenced to soothe White comfort. Was the goal to tell the unfiltered truth about racism in America or to make those listening feel comfortable? I landed somewhere in the middle. Even as a I chose a preferred landing, I knew that if I said nothing, that too would be acceptable.

My own discomfort wasn't only in the context of my commentary, but it was in that moment that I realized the length of time I had gone without using my own voice to remind Black and Brown people of this providence I had come to embrace. I realized there was another conversation happening in these communities to which I had become disconnected. But I fear I'm not alone; White spaces have been the burial ground for many Black voices. Many Black voices, similar to my own, are buried and muffled in their current context. They want to speak, but they can't do this authentically. If they do, they run the risk of being labeled angry, disgruntled, and problematic.

As the number of Black Methodist congregations continues to close or decline, many of my colleagues will be called to lead and serve in White congregations. Many of these same congregations will take advantage of this decline to help diversify their own staff. However, there is a difference in welcoming Black faces and embracing Black voices. Black faces will add more diversity to the website and brochures. Garnering the right faces will be the low-hanging fruit. But if we offer our faces, can we also bring our voices? Can we bring our voices even if it makes some feel uncomfortable? Can we affirm that our lives matter even if it offends others in the congregation? Can we bring our compassion and our rage? Can we bring our tears of joy and sorrow? Are we able to speak authentically to the emptiness and the darkness in every facet of the surrounding community (even if it's one that's too close for comfort)? Can we publicly affirm that our lives matter? If we choose to give our faces to White spaces, we should not have to make concession with our voices. I could be alone, but in choosing this journey, I should not have to also abandon speaking to various communities that desperately need to see leaders who recognize their voices as well.

We are at a critical turning point in our nation's history and in our denomination. History will judge our works by examining what we did and said during these turbulent times. The middle ground has been canceled as a viable option. Similar to the congregation that I presently serve, White voices and congregations are entering into the conversation. The bending of our moral consciousness as a nation and Christian faith will require courageous voices that are committed to intentional persistence. The future of the denomination and the moral consciousness of our nation depend on authentic Black voices. As the nation becomes more diverse, our voices are needed for such a time as this. Genesis reminds us we must choose to speak, because there is power in our voices can give light to darkness. They can transform impossibilities. They have the power to give life. I stutter. I wish I didn't, but I do. I've learned that it takes courage to speak. I'm Black, I'm Christian, I'm Methodist, and I choose to use my voice.

Chapter Eight

I'M BLACK. I'M QUEER LESBIAN. I'M METHODIST. I'M THRIVING, IRREGARDLESS.

Pamela R. Lightsey

Dean of the Faculty and VP of Student Affairs,
Meadville Lombard Theological School

Liberation

It's a mystery, a profound and deep mystery how African Americans, after two and a half centuries of slavery, another century of lynching and Jim Crow segregation, and yet still come out loving White people!

—James Cone, *Said I Wasn't Gonna Tell Nobody:*
The Making of a Black Theologian

On a hot, muggy Florida day on April 29, 2012, I sat among an audience of LGBTQ United Methodists listening to a speech presented by a scholar whose work had significantly affected my life, ministry, and academic journey: James H. Cone. He came to our General Conference held in Tampa, at the invitation of a collaborative network of LGBTQ and affirming agencies then known as "Love Your Neighbor Coalition." The title and theme of his speech were the same used in his then most recent (2011) publication, *The Cross snd The Lynching Tree.* For thirty-eight minutes, Professor Cone held court, leading his listeners through a resplendent theological and historical exploration of the nature and impact of racism upon enslaved Africans and their progeny. As we listened, I marveled at the wholesome responses from Black attendees, the expressions of gratitude from almost all present, and even the blank stares by some, as if they were wondering, "What has this subject to do with LGBTQ oppression within The United Methodist Church?"

Years later, I stood in the middle of a convention-area hallway between the many sessions of an American Academy of Religion annual meeting, receiving a congratulatory hug from Professor Cone as he thanked me for writing *Our Lives Matter: A Womanist Queer Theology.* Frankly, I thought he would not even know me. "Of course, I know you! I'm using your book in one of my classes!" he said in such a matter-of-fact way.

I had cited James Cone in paperwork I submitted for review and approval to the Order of Elders in The United Methodist Church. Despite being cautioned against utilizing Black liberation theology in my paperwork for the Order of Deacons (I was ordained a "deacon on the elders' track" in 1999), I staunchly argued my theological perspectives by utilizing the work of many liberation scholars, including James Cone. I was affirmed for ordination by the Board of Ordained Ministry, but I was soon to experience the kind of bigotry that my professors and scholars like Dr. Cone knew all too well.

I received a call from my district superintendent one day prior to ordination as a deacon. At the time, I was in my second year of master of divinity studies. After exchanging perfunctory southern pleasantries, the district superintendent stated the purpose of his call with the kind of myopic arrogance I'd become accustomed to growing up during the years of Jim Crow laws. "Well, I cun getcha ordaynd," he said in a deep White southern drawl. "But I don' have uh Black chuch to put ya' in. So you gon' need to check 'roun' sum uh dem Black chuches neah ya' school to see if any one of dem can fit ya' in. Den let me know and I'll make sho' we getcha an appointment to one of dem whilst ya' finish up school." Long silence on my part as I recalled our denomination's polity contained in the *Book of Discipline*.

During those seconds that seemed like minutes, I recalled debates I'd had as a student of Bishop L. Scott Allen, the last bishop elected in the former Methodist Central Jurisdiction. Bishop Allen was at that time our professor of United Methodist polity. As a feisty senior, Bishop Allen was a man who didn't suffer fools gladly.[79] After many years in retirement at the time, this episcopal leader was revered by many for his astute observations of even the most minor details of the *Book of Discipline*. I counted it a win whenever I was able to excel in answering a question he put to me during class. My head swelled with joy on those few occasions when I was also able to respectfully correct his interpretation of denominational law. I put in many hours of study simply to prepare for our weekly one-and-a-half-hour class. I was humbled to receive a scholarship in Bishop Scott's name at the end of that semester.

79. The negative phrasing of Paul's words contained in 2 Corinthians 11:19, "Because you, who are so wise, are happy to put up with fools."

Having proverbially sat at the feet of this great giant in the denomination, I wondered silently during my conversation with the district superintendent why he was the one making an offer of an appointment when only bishops had the final say on the subject. And what about the guaranteed appointment system? Those thoughts paled in comparison to a knee-jerk response running through my mind: Why is this White man trying to segregate me in the ministry of the church? I never asked to be placed in a Black church. I thought Methodists believed the world was our pulpit! Why can't I be appointed to ANY available church as senior or associate pastor?

Ultimately, without even so much as a phone call with the bishop of our annual conference, I was given a part-time appointment serving as an assistant to the senior pastor at the church where I and my children had been attending since returning to the continental United States of America. Years later, after receiving a PhD, I went to lecture at a Southern annual conference where a clergy colleague said to me after introducing me, "I don't know how we let you get away!" This time, rather than a silent conversation in my head, I was able to fold my response into my lecture. The answer was and still remains a plain and simple truth: Racism was a first cause. Homophobia was also co-constitutive element of what threatened my capacity to thrive in ministry in that annual conference.

Thriving is a way of being, which is the theme for this chapter. Perhaps some readers will interpret this entire book as a Black Liberation apologetic with specific attention paid to the ministry of Black people within The United Methodist Church. An apologetic is not my aim. I agree with Toni Morrison:

The function, the very serious function of racism . . . is distraction. I*t keeps you from doing your work*. It keeps you explaining over and over again, your reason for being. Somebody says you have no language and you spend 20 years proving that you do. Somebody says your head isn't shaped properly so you have scientists working on the fact that it is. Somebody says that you have no art so you dredge that up. Somebody says that you have no kingdoms and, so you dredge that up.

None of this is necessary.

There will always be *one more thing*.[80]

I won't be explaining Black people's reason for being in America or this denomination. Instead, I have three matters to explore. What does it mean to embrace ontological Blackness (or African American identity) in a world and in a denomination filled with anti-Blackness and anti-queerness? What is this work of embracing Blackness, not with the goal of defending Blackness against racism or in contrast to Whiteness, but instead to let it stand, to walk in it as a disposition, a distinct attribute for a particular people?

The fact of our oppression has been told over and over again. I'm now more interested in how an oppressed people embraced and loved itself, irregardless of the metanarratives that function to uplift White supremacy at the expense of other racial categories, particularly Blackness.

Second, leading up to the election of President Trump, my journey within The United Methodist Church convinced me that the Christian movement of our era is in real need of divine transformation. Readers of this chapter will take in my analysis of contemporary Christianity and juxtaposition of it (in general terms)

80. Toni Morrison, "A Humanist View," speech given at Portland State University, May 30, 1975. Transcription by Keisha E. McKenzie, Auburn Seminary https://www.mackenzian.com/wp-content/uploads/2014/07/Transcript_Portland State_TMorrison.pdf.

with what we have come to believe of the prophetic ministry of Jesus of Nazareth.

This unpacking of where we are over and against the aspirational, what is possible for us, is how I regard Black people's resources for not merely surviving but thriving, irregardless. I regard these resources for thriving as my liberationist heirloom specifically to Black—including Black LGBTQ—people but more broadly to those for whom the admonition to "to do justice, embrace faithful love, and walk humbly with your God" (Mic 6:8) still serves as a daily way of being.

The Hog in the Spring

A man was wandering in the hills and in the woods and he was looking for a spring that was supposed to have clear water where he could get a drink because he was thirsty, very thirsty. And he found a spring that was very muddy and dirty and filthy, the water wasn't clear, so he began to sit down and try to get in some clear, clean water by trying to clear the spring out. He went through all kind of hassles and changes trying to clear the spring out, so he can get a clear drink of water from the spring. And another man came along and said, "What are you trying to do?" He said, "I'm trying to get a clear drink of water here, I've been thirsty for a long, long time, and I can't seem to get the dirt and the filth and the mud and the dirt that's here in this spring cleared out to get me a clear drink of water." The man said, "Well the reason you can't do that," he says, "is because on top of the hill about a mile or two back where you haven't checked out yet," he says, "there's a hog in the spring." He says, "there's a hog in the spring, and a lot of those pigs are running around too in the spring." All we want is a little freedom, all we want is a clear drink of water, but there's a hog in the spring![81]

---

81. Untitled speech given by Bobby Seale on April 16, 1968, at the Kaleidoscope Theater, in Los Angeles, California. http://americanradioworks.publicradio.org/features/Blackspeech/bseale.html.

I love this parable because it demonstrates how we far too often handle complex problems. It's easy enough to go at the thing that is right before us, which we think we have the capacity to control, when the problem is outside our immediate view, situated at a distant periphery affecting the quotidian details of our lives.

For centuries, since Africans were captured, taken from their homeland, and enslaved in America—a land stolen from Native Americans by the same colonizing people—African Americans have wrestled against a metanarrative that ascribed their Blackness as the source of their own oppression. The basic persistent tale argues, "The Negro being Black is because he is cursed by God."[82] If we go at this thing, this ongoing racist trope in its many forms, I fear we may be blinded to the hog in the spring. I'm not of the mind that the hog is racism. The source of the dirt—dirt that is racism—as ubiquitous as it may seem, is not a hog called White supremacy, or Blackness, homophobia, transphobia, sexism, or a hog called classism, as easy as it may be to make any of those arguments. Rather, the source of the dirt is hubris. Hubris is the hog rolling around in the cool, flowing spring waters from which we yearn to take a clean refreshing drink for our souls.

Certainly, if we expand this imagery, we can set the stage for any number of other bigotries, from which we must purify the water before safely drinking. Though the preacher in me is tempted, the point of this chapter is best upheld by unpacking the influence of hubris.[83]

---

82. See the speeches of Fundamentalist Church of Jesus Christ of Latter-Day Saints leader Warren Jeffs.. Also see interpretations of Judaic Oral Torah accounts of the Curse of Ham and the Hamitic Hypothesis.

83. One might even say it is either irony or hubris that I seem to be advancing a type of ontological argument for the existence of Blackness.

In his *Systematic Theology*, Paul Tillich defined hubris as "the self-elevation of man into the sphere of the divine."[84] Hubris is the first sin of humanity; that which estranged humanity from God and, what is more, from one another. The sin of hubris is foremost, the centering and lifting up of one's self in contrast to all others, including God, the Creator. Hubris is not confined to individual sin but is also collective, cultural. Elsewhere I write that "when hubris is at work humanity is conscious of that presence not as the center of our lives but as an appendage of our lives. Once the human situation and relationship with God has shifted in this way, self-elevation and indeed marginalization of others inevitably results."[85]

In arguing that hubris is the source (the hog) of all oppression we can then look at White supremacy as but one expression of hubris among many, albeit the most dangerous of our time. This, for me, leads to the question: why embrace Blackness rather than simply advocating for the sacredness of humanity? Surely, that is my heart's desire. However, to do so in this era would be tantamount to the current "All Lives Matter" response. While it is logically true, it is not realistically the case.

At this time, persons identified by the racial construct as Black are being verbally and physically attacked and discriminated against in ways many thought our nation had long gotten past. While it has become en vogue to talk about race as a social construct, I have a sort of disdain for that entire conversation because it tends to revel too much in science rather than deal with the impact of the social function of racism. That is, I seek

84. Paul Tillich, *Systematic Theology*, vol. 3 (Chicago: University of Chicago Press, 1963), 50.

85. Pamela Lightsey, *Our Lives Matter: A Womanist Queer Theology* (Eugene, OR: Wipf & Stock, 2015), 61.

to understand, not to yet again explain, but to understand this distraction for Black people and this violent disposition for White people.

There is no way that I can fully understand what makes any White person—Christian or not—behave violently against Black people, though many books have been written about the matter. Instead, I think it's far more interesting to think about the beauty and strength of a people who have cast off the American Dream; that place where all people are equal and have the same fundamental opportunities and access to achieve that elusive ideal for "whatever you set your mind to."

To walk with this mindset, to shed this notion of any type of truth to this mythical American Dream has been a way of embracing our Black beingness rather than being subsumed under and by the contradictions of this national ethos. I think of Audre Lorde's conversation with James Baldwin as a great example. Bearing in her body a multiplicity of oppressions, Lorde talks to Baldwin about how she was thriving against what she called "the deep horror of even our different nightmares," among them being the American Dream.

> Deep, deep, deep down I know that dream was never mine. And I wept and I cried, and I fought, and I stormed, but I just knew it. I was Black. I was female. And I was out—out—by any construct wherever the power lay. So, if I had to claw myself insane, if I lived, I was going to have to do it alone. Nobody was dreaming about me. Nobody was even studying me except as something to wipe out.[86]

86. "Revolutionary Hope: A Conversation between James Baldwin and Audre Lorde," *Essence Magazine*, 1984.

Similar to Lorde, many Black United Methodists know very well that for all its talks, for all its "acts of repentance" the dream of full inclusion in the denomination is not yet ours. What is more, because the denomination—the institutional church—is but a macro-level entity of society at large, itself at the cusp of schism, Black people may actually never experience full inclusion in the denomination. One has but to look at the Protocol of Reconciliation and Grace through Separation,[87] the plan for an amenable parting of the ways of the denomination's more conservative (called Traditionalist) members from whatever remains of its body.

The plan admits to "the historical role of the Methodist movement in systems of systematic racial violence, exploitation and discrimination." To their credit, its authors responded to the insistence of many UMC leaders, me included, that the church not only acknowledge its role in discrimination but that it offer support to churches whose members are predominantly of those "Asian, Black, Hispanic-Latino, Native American and Pacific Islander communities." Though some may celebrate the carving out of funding specifically targeted for these "communities historically marginalized by the sin of racism" it is but a paltry sum being contributed across an eight-year span.

I wonder about the capacity for thriving and not merely surviving for Black people in our denomination or whatever is to become of it. To that end, Lorde's words resonate with me. "If I lived, I was going to have to do it alone." Must we eke out our survival alone? Fortunately, that has not been the case. Even dur-

87.   The current "Protocol of Reconciliation and Grace through Separation," https://www.unitedmethodistbishops.org/files/websites/www/pdfs/signed+umc +mediation+protocoal+statement+-2020.pdf.

ing the pandemic, fellow Americans of diverse cultures, including many White allies, have taken to the streets to protest excessive police abuse against Black people. That notwithstanding, with the increased visibility and activity of White supremacist gangs, Black people's very lives are under constant threat. We are not imagining that threat, for according to DHS Deputy Secretary Ken Cuccinelli, not only does White supremacy exist, its followers—when violent—strike at deadly levels.

> I have no qualms criticizing the White supremacy threat, neither does the Secretary, neither does the Department of Homeland Security. And we recognize when those people act out violently that they're uh, they show the highest level of lethality, meaning if you compare the number of violent incidents to the number of deaths, the number of deaths relative to the incidents is very high compared to other types of threats.[88]

It's no coincidence that this rise in violence took place under the Trump administration, given his penchant for stoking the flames of racist discord. He is the antithesis of ethical leadership, who has located his clan among evangelical Christians, not surprisingly a base that includes United Methodist members, such as former Attorney General Jefferson Beauregard Sessions III, and Nikki Haley, former ambassador to the United Nations. Trump's vitriol is not a surprising anomaly but a part of the continued trajectory of bigotry within Christianity in general and United Methodism specifically.

Why is it not surprising? Because, The United Methodist Church has, like other predominantly White denominations, always had within its membership persons willing to do harm and

---

88. Kenneth Cuccinelli, interview by Hallie Jackson, MSNBC September 4, 2020.

willing to close their eyes to harm done to Black people. In one of its first General Conferences after the merger creating The UMC, held in 1972, the Rev. Gil Caldwell[89] stepped to the microphone to address the delegates as they were gathered in the Civic Center in Atlanta, Georgia. Recognizing the steady existence of racism within the denomination, he spoke these strong words:

> It is quite possible then that some of you find yourselves saying in these moments that here they go again. And you have turned off your psychological hearing aids, you have put on your blinders, you have readjusted the rose-colored glasses. Some of you are saying that "you are hurting your cause," and yet if you say this, you are standing in a significant company of American people, for they said that you remember . . . a lot of people said that Malcolm X was hurting the cause, and a lot of people said that Martin Luther King was hurting the cause. And, yet somehow in their death, some of these same persons recognized the validity of their cause and pretend they are staunch supporters.[90]

As it was in those days, so it is today: The United Methodist Church is filled with pretenders who say they love Black people but whose works are far from it! You can't love Black people, and support and vote for a man who has led this nation to the brink of fascism, and who has egged on violence against Black people. Moreover, you can't love Black people and advocate for laws within our *Book of Discipline* that continue discrimination against LGBTQ persons, since there are also scores of Black

89. I learned of the death of my friend and dear mentor Rev. Caldwell as I was finishing this chapter. He was a man who believed deeply in civil rights and served as an elder statesman of the movement in the 1960s, marching alongside Martin Luther King Jr. By taking civil rights seriously, in his later years he championed the rights of LGBTQ persons within society and our denomination. We owe a great debt to this man, and I shall be forever grateful to have had the opportunity to work alongside him advancing the cause of liberation for all God's creation.

90. *Journal of the 1972 General Conference of The United Methodist Church*, https://archive.org/stream/journalatlantal01unit/journalatlantal01unit_djvu.txt.

LGBTQ members within the denomination. It is a remarkable piece of alchemy by which White people embrace legislation that harms Black, Brown, Asian, and Native Americans as well as immigrants then proclaim Christianity on Sunday morning. For these reasons the Christian movement of our era, if it is to remain efficacious, must undergo a serious transformation, a divine metamorphosis, if you will.

The priestly and prophetic ministry of Jesus is the salvific elixir and only cure for the institutional church. Indeed, since its beginnings, it has been understood that the righteousness of the institutional church will only be real and present among its members when every inch of its hierarchy and body yields to the gospel of Jesus, the Christ. I'm not convinced, by the history of the Church universal, that it has ever met that standard. I'm clear that there have been epochal moments when its local churches and members have come remarkably close. What is more, those moments have taken shape when churches attended to and advocated for the well-being and liberation of oppressed persons, the poor, the stranger, and the sick. This is, in fact, the ministerial example that Jesus left the church and the tradition taken up by the early "hush harbor" gatherings of African people in America.

I write about not only survival but thriving as a Black queer lesbian Christian within The United Methodist Church because I have been able to tap into a quality of life and spirituality developed by my ancestors who, against all odds, survived and thrived the indecencies, the daily torture of being an enslaved people living in these continental United States. The narratives of Jesus's life and ministry—as they derived it—was the source of survival techniques for life in the wilderness that was slavocracy. The hush harbor tradition and the emergent Black independent (free) churches also, through the lens of Jesus's life and ministry, provided Black adherents skills for thriving regardless of the oppression invoked through Jim Crow laws.

In Jesus, Black Christians saw someone who loved all people and knew that they ought to comport themselves likewise. He was in fellowship with the sinners of his day and those considered righteous. Thus, Black Christians, against even common logic so often have attempted to love even the mutant strand of Christianity embodied in evangelical believers who supported Trump and his policies. It remains, as James Cone said in his memoir, "a mystery, a profound and deep mystery!"

I certainly hope that The United Methodist Church of the future will be able to cut through the tentacles of its own racism and concomitant bigotries. It's not enough to be clean of one manner of structural oppression. If it is to survive it must undergo a deep purge of its soul, a thorough cleansing far more glorious than even the commander Naaman's healing. Not only the flesh—the outer bounds of the denomination, being its members—needs healing but especially within its very soul, meaning its ethos and polity. In the meantime, it seems more beneficial to address the mechanisms, the resources that I believe have been and will continue to be helpful for Black people regardless of the vicissitudes of life. First, a few statistics.

The unemployment rate of Black Americans remains nearly double that of White workers. In fact, the current gap is the widest it's been since May 2015. In August 2020 the unemployment rate for Black workers was at 13 percent and for White workers at 7.3 percent.[91] "The gap is now the widest since May 2015 and

---

91.   U.S. Bureau of Labor Statistics, "Economic News Release," https://www .bls.gov/news.release/empsit.t02.htm.

exposes an important economic component of racial inequality at a pivotal moment in U.S. race relations."[92] It's a foregone conclusion that Black families have significantly lower wealth than White families. Frankly, that is the case for Brown, Asian, and Native American families as well. White median household income has continued to outpace other groups and has little to do with individual achievement and more to do with structural racism. When it comes to education, "Black students are much less likely to graduate from high school and attend college than White students with the same family income."[93] And finally, the disparities in COVID-19—related deaths, particularly the higher death rate among Black people, will be the subject of medical studies for years to come. "African Americans in Illinois, as an example, account for 17 percent of confirmed COVID-19 cases and 29.7 percent of attributed deaths, they make up only 15 percent of the state's population."[94]

These tragic facts are indicative of how truly devastating structural racism is on Black people in general. What these statistics do not tell is how Black Christians in this era will continue to sustain their resilience. What resources will they tap into beyond the walls and sacred text of the church?

92. Jonnell Marte, "Gap in U.S. Black and White Unemployment Rates Is Widest in Five Years," *Reuters*, July 2, 2020, https://www.reuters.com/article /us-usa-economy-unemployment-race/gap-in-us-Black-and-White-unemployment -rates-is-widest-in-five-years-idUSKBN2431X7.

93. Matt Barnum, "Race, Not Just Poverty, Shapes Who Graduates in America And Other Education Lessons from a Big New Study," https://www.chalkbeat .org/2018/3/23/21104601/race-not-just-poverty-shapes-who-graduates-in-ameri ca-and-other-education-lessons-from-a-big-new-stu.

94. Gunther Eysenbach, ed., "Why African Americans Are a Potential Target for COVID-19 Infection in the United States," National Center for Biotechnology Information, June 12, 2020, https://www.ncbi.nlm.nih.gov/pmc/articles /PMC7294999/.

Heirloom

The word *heirloom* comes to mind during the imposed isolation of COVID-19. The skills for survival and thriving have been passed on as valuable heirlooms to me and other Black people from our ancestors. Those heirlooms are passed on generally in unremarkable yet repetitive actions, conversations, lyrics, even idioms across Black culture. For instance, I think of the lessons learned as I sat on the floor between my mother's legs while she combed through my thick hair, parting it, scratching and conditioning my scalp, then plaiting it up. Several times through the year after plaiting my hair, she would cut and collect the damaged ends then burn them in the ashtray and instruct me on how to dispose of the ashes and why this ritual was important. That was always a special time, and it remains a joyous memory to strengthen my resolve against oppression.

This example becomes a liberationist heirloom because the lessons that were passed on were conveyed in both the quotidian and the seasonal events of my life. Liberationist heirlooms are passed on quietly and at times in the very presence of anti-Black racists. They happen as rituals, as teachable moments, as cultural representations of the strength and subversive techniques that have been employed by Black people. These liberationist heirlooms are countercultural traditions in predominantly White contexts. I regard them as the mores that span across time and geographical contexts, within which Black communities are situated.

The liberationist heirlooms of my elders (examples include Gil Caldwell, Melvin Talbert, Katie Cannon, Kate McClary, my aunts Mary and Lillian) enabled me to thrive in The United Methodist Church irregardless of its racism and discriminatory laws against LGBTQ persons. Sometimes these teachings have been straightforward, sometimes subtle; sometimes intentional and some quite unintentional. These heirlooms help me hold my head up even when cast as a recalcitrant sinner. They help me hold on to the faith that has been transmuted to me by my ancestors.

As I find myself now seen as an elder among Black LGBTQ activists within and outside the denomination, I have made a commitment to mentoring and passing on ways of being that will help Black and Brown students survive, thrive, and eventually overcome oppression. I'm assiduously working to disengage myself from the ways that Whiteness shows up in my scholarship, ministry, and activism. I keep on faith because above all, I believe in the beauty of Black people in all our variegated shades, textures, and expressions.

I trust that by God's help and the liberationist heirlooms given me by my elders that my capacity to survive and thrive as a Black queer lesbian ordained elder and constructive theologian of The United Methodist Church will serve as a guiding healing vector now and in the years to come. As it is, I'm content to be among a people and their allies who, as the ultimate act of resistance, are determined, come what may, to maintain that inexplicable Spirit-given joie de vivre , irregardless.

Chapter Nine

I'M BLACK. I'M CONSCIOUS.
I'M YOUR CONSCIENCE.

F. Willis Johnson

Lead Pastor, Living Tree Church, Columbus, Ohio

I'm Black. I'm Christian. I'm Methodist, and constant is the struggle to define and remain answerable to one's authentic self. Slavery, segregation, and oppression are undeniably a part of the African diaspora and American story. Being Black in America means you live under a genocidal threat. Being Black in United Methodism requires filtering Western philosophical, anthropological, theological, political, and cultural practices through a hermeneutic of suspicion.

I'm Black. I'm conscious. I'm your conscience. These declarative statements acknowledge how I name myself, and how others in American society perceive me. Inherent in each statement is criticism, protest, and an appeal addressed to particular persons or groups. These deeply personal declarations shape an open letter to a people with hardened hearts, closed minds, and separate doors.

The accumulation of microaggressions—daily imposition of systemic economic, social, and political inequities—experienced in church and society perpetually undermines and reminds Black

123

and "othered" folk that they are "less than." The identity of Black persons, especially in religious life, has always been a binary proposition. Black Methodists are often forced to discern and decide to compromise or suppress important parts of themselves. Being Black in United Methodism requires reconciling one's Black identity with one's Wesleyan history.

Historical Perspective

Africans and African Americans are integral to the history and future of Methodist life in America. In 1758 John Wesley baptized his first Black convert. In his manuscript, "Rediscovering the African American Heritage of The United Methodist Church," Elliot Wright revisited the record of African American presence and importance within the Protestant brand of Methodism. "Persons of African American descent were numerous and visible 225 years ago," according to Wright. "But these facts were often glossed over in ensuing years, especially in the early nineteenth century as slavery became a major issue of conflict in politics and religion"[95]; hence, the split among Methodists along geographical and philosophical lines in 1845 over slavery.

Black folks were Methodist before 1968. Before United Methodism was ever imagined, Black folk possessed Wesleyan roots since the beginning of the revival movement. For example, in the 1760s laypersons, inclusive of Black men and women regardless of their slave status, initiated the first American

95.   Elliot Wright, "Recovering the African American Heritage of The United Methodist," March 2, 2010.

Methodist Societies.[96] Yet, the presence of Black folks remains an anomaly in Methodism.

John and Charles Wesley deserve credit for sowing the seeds that bloomed into Methodism, but the history of Methodism in America is a compromised story of a fledgling nation forged in the crucible of Whiteness. Among American Methodists, the story of the Wesley brothers is a familiar one. Both men were missionaries commissioned from the Church of England to serve in the colony of Georgia, and arriving there in 1736. Despite the brothers' unsuccessful missionary efforts and subsequent return to England, the spirit of Methodism was not dead.

Historians often romanticize John and Charles Wesley for leading a renewal movement within the Church of England, so that their teachings spread to the American colonies through Methodist immigrants from England. The result was a lay-led movement that championed and organized Methodist classes and congregations in America.

"Wesley was always reaching out to those who were different," quips Methodist scholar Lovett H. Weems, who notes that

> diversity was a challenge for [John Wesley] and early Methodists.
> . . . The results make clear the seriousness with which he took the
> task. Wesley sought out those who were different socially and eco-
> nomically. He especially sought a church open to sinners who felt
> rejected by society and God. "Outcasts" of all, "to you I call," he says
> in a hymn. God's arms are spread "t'embrace you all."[97]

The spirit of Wesley was embraced and enhanced by early American missionaries as they cast their nets in hopes of attracting

---

96. F. Douglas Powe, "Historical Roots of Just-Us," in *Just Us or Justice: Moving toward a Pan-Methodist Theology* (Nashville: Abingdon Press, 2009), 31.

97. Lovett H. Weems, *Leadership in the Wesleyan Spirit* (Nashville: Abingdon Press, 1999), 96.

all persons. Methodism had a strange and warm attraction among African Americans. Nathan Hatch explains, "More African Americans became Christians in ten years of Methodist preaching than in a century of Anglican."[98]African descendants continued their participation among Methodist circles despite the divisive 1845 split between states in the North and South.

As once-separate Methodist factions began to reconcile, a compromise developed at the 1939 reunion that established the all-Black, nongeographical Central Jurisdiction. The Central Jurisdiction was established in four areas, with a fifth added in 1960, and lasted until its abolishment in 1968, the same year the Methodists and Evangelical United Brethren merged to form The United Methodist Church.

In *Segregation of The Methodist Church Polity: Reform Movements that Ended Racial Segregation*, Black Methodist pioneer W. Astor Kirk wrote:

> Only a few people know that the Methodist Church/United Methodist Church was once formally and constitutionally racially segregated. Many who have heard of the Central Jurisdiction Organization assumed it to be a Black denomination, like the African Methodist Episcopal Church or the African Methodist Episcopal Zion Church.

Despite systemic segregation, many Blacks within Methodism remained a part of the church. Wright addresses the perennial question among church historians: why did any people of African descent seek to remain connected to The Methodist Episcopal Church? He notes that initial attraction to Methodist practice was principally the reason for their enduring connectivity to The

98.   Nation Hatch quoted in H. W. Bowden and P. C. Kemeny, *American Church History: A Reader* (Nashville: Abingdon Press, 1998), 284.

Methodist Episcopal Church. However, with reference to work of Lewis V. Baldwin, Wright directs us to five reasons why both slaves and free Blacks gravitated to American Methodism:

1. The revival style and ethos of the movement allowed for freedom of expression and resembled African religious traditions.

2. The message was simple and clear, with an emphasis on love and hope.

3. Methodism, despite its failure to effectively oppose slavery, had an egalitarian impulse, and it was accessible, even to those held in slavery.

4. Methodist preachers actively evangelized among African Americans.

5. Blacks themselves were a "dynamic force" in attracting others.[99]

John H. Wigger, cited by Wright, observes that African descendants were first responders to the gospel message shared by Methodist missionaries:

> The participation of persons often described as "poor Blacks" in Methodist worship was reported by the first preachers sent by founder John Wesley to the American colonies. The journal entries of early missionary preachers denotes African descendants as "poor Blacks."[100]

---

99. Wright, "Recovering the African American Heritage of The United Methodist."

100. Wright, "Recovering the African American Heritage of The United Methodist."

The characterization of African descendants as "poor Blacks" endures and carries a negative connotation concerning the cultural, social, political, and spiritual worth of African Americans. The adjective is consistent with how Eurocentric and colonizing cultures devalue others, especially people of the African Diaspora. Moreover, a segmented, racist pathology taints, suppresses, and questions the spiritual acumen of Africans and African Americans. Fortunately scholars such as Will Gravel are studying the influential work of the Holy Spirit (pneumatology) among African Americans as found in the journals of early preachers.[101]

The American Methodist Church's history and attitude concerning racial equity remain weak. The pace of change for racial equity in the church continually lags behind the larger society. The United Methodist Church, while striving, still struggles in its efforts to dismantle the racially motivated systems that exist within its connection. Hence, the Black experience in Methodism continues to require a coalition of affinity groups, resources, and spaces that are affirming and empowering.

Our Predicament

Black churches were founded in response to anti-Black hatred, suppression, and terrorism. By default and for its survival any given Black church had to be different and responsive to a wide range of social and economic threats to the well-being of the individual. Albert J. Raboteau writes:

> The history of African-American religion exemplifies America's long and dramatic engagement with ethnic pluralism and the central role

101. Wright, "Recovering the African American Heritage of The United Methodist."

of race in shaping American life. Thousands of Africans from diverse cultures and religious traditions, forcibly transported to America as slaves, retained many African customs even as they converted to Christianity. Before and after the Civil War, African-Americans drew religion to its moral and prophetic calling making it the center not only of African-American culture but a challenging ethic of equality and dignity throughout American society.[102]

The echoes of the Black Lives Matter protest movement reverberate in and around us daily. These spiritual, often invisible pulses, are evident at the site of another death in real-time lament and resistance, in hollering and protest. William McClain in his historic work asserts that Black folk are the primordial conscience of Methodism.[103] Contemporary examples of Black Methodist faith communities bearing the burden of the nation's moral conscience include Ferguson, Baltimore's Sandtown, and Mother Emanuel African Methodist Episcopal Church, in Charleston, South Carolina, site of the 2015 racially motivated mass shooting. Originally formed as Hampstead Church, which was founded by former Black congregants in Charleston's three White Methodist Episcopal churches.

#Ferguson became a buzzword for some of this nation's worst racial profiling and inequality. The streets of Ferguson, for me and many other Black Methodists, became a civic laboratory—our front line and our sanctuary. It may have seemed to some in 2014 that this was the powder keg, the moment when change would somehow alight on us from above. It is clear now that Ferguson is one leg of the long relay route toward equity and justice in

102.   A. J. Raboteau, *Canaan Land: A Religious History of African Americans* (New York: Oxford University Press, 2001), ix.
103.   William B. McClain, *Black People in The Methodist Church: Whither Thou Goest?* (Nashville: Abingdon Press, 1990), 90.

America, a run of civilization-defining consequence that began in 1619 when the slaves were driven ashore by guards with weapons.

Again we are forced to learn the names of Black individuals killed at the hands of our police guardians. We stand at a fork in the road, to make another decision about whether to divide our allegiance concerning new forms of oppressive othering. Across the "connection" cabinets and jurisdictions wrestle with the perennial question of the pan-Wesleyan church, "What shall we do with the Blacks or othered?" As always, except for a well-written letter or prayer, the official United Methodist Church has a disposition entrenched in Whiteness and largely remains silent, inactive, about the mounting death toll of Black folk murdered in the streets of America, or it resorts to further marginalization and isolation of those who cause discomfort through their Black presence or lived experience.[104] Far too often, the response from our United Methodist connection, from the episcopacy, general agencies, conferences, and local leaders is slow and low, or absent altogether.

At this point, silence no longer signals discernment or political correctness. Silence is instead abuse. Silence in the face of such egregious violence, in light of such apparent injustice, is a decision to turn mute or render another's reality invisible. It is a choice to maintain comfort and decorum over the lives of our brothers and sisters. It willingly allows this pattern of disrespect for human life to continue. This silence is unloving. It is selfish. It is cowardice. Silence in the face of injustice and death is not Christlike and is an affront to our Methodist heritage. Truth told, large swaths of church sit both silent and idle during periods of war, political

104. Powe, *Just Us or Justice*, 81.

and social maleficence, slavery, civil rights, and Black nationalist periods—and right now!

Every fatal encounter between citizens and police undresses the scabbed-over remnants of a deep abrasion my family and my community experienced in August 2014 in Ferguson. The political pandering and pseudo-intellectual prognosticating, seemingly nonstop racist rants, and looped footage of brutality and dehumanization pains my heart and pricks my soul. These emotional and spiritual electric shocks serve as constant reminders that my community, my family, and my body are Black in America. My awareness of this, combined with suspicion about White allegiance to a dystopian form of democracy, does not mean that I'm unpatriotic. It should not result in bastardization of my civil liberties or raise questions of my adherence to faith.

Silence is no longer an option. We are past the point of discussion regarding the particularities of individual shootings. We have exceeded the statute of limitations for mere collegial conversation that fails to wholly address prejudice, misinformation, or even hate in order to avoid discomfort or offense. Holy conferencing and huddling is not stopping folks from getting killed for doing what they are either instructed or constitutionally afforded an opportunity to do. Neither are such covenantal acts furthering Jesus's true message, nor are they reflective of his unconditional love or equitable acts. It is time to speak up; to stand up and act up!

In his "Letter from a Birmingham Jail," Martin Luther King Jr. laments "the white moderate who is more devoted to 'order' than to justice . . . who constantly says 'I agree with you in the goal you seek, but I can't agree with your methods of direct action.'"[105]

Our religious institutions have remained moderate for far too long. It's time to do more, to expect more from our church and our leaders. As Christians our intervention can no longer be delayed by our handicaps framed in questions of "what do I say or do?" Each of us must self-determine to consciously commit to admitting our shortcomings, intentionally engaging in turning away from our sins, and moving toward wholeness.

The United Methodist Social Principles claim:

> We affirm all persons as equally valuable in the sight of God. We therefore work toward societies in which each person's value is recognized, maintained, and strengthened. . . . We deplore acts of hate or violence against groups or persons based on race, color, national origin, ethnicity, age, gender, disability, status, economic condition, sexual orientation, gender identity, or religious affiliation.[106]

The problem is that while we disavow acts of hate and violence in principle, we remain silent or passive when confronted by hate and violence.

According to a Pew Research study conducted in 2014, United Methodists are one of the least diverse religious groups in the United States. While this study may have failed to take into account the transcontinental nature of our church, it raises an interesting question: How has one of the largest mainline

105. The complete letter is archived at http://okra.stanford.edu/transcription /document_images/undecided/630416-019.pdf; King's recording of the letter is found at http://okra.stanford.edu/transcription/audio/630416001.mp3.

106. "Social Principles: The Social Community," The Book of Discipline of The United Methodist Church--2016 (Nashville: The United Methodist Publishing House), https://www.umc.org/en/content/social-principles-the-social-commu nity. https://www.umc.org/en/content/social-principles-the-social-community.

denominations and leading proponents of social holiness maintained institutional Whiteness?[107]

It's no secret that United Methodist leaders have struggled with fully incorporating those who are non-White into the life of the church. Toni Morrison reminds us, "In this country, American means White. Everybody else has to hyphenate." Consider the formation of several other denominations, which we now describe as Pan-Methodists, who have their origins in The Methodist Episcopal Church and Methodist Episcopal Church, South. By failing to fully embrace its Black brothers and sisters, these two denominations left a stain that we have yet to recover from. Imagine the level of true diversity that we could boast if the members of St. George's MEC had acknowledged the sacred worth of Richard Allen and his colleagues, inviting them down to sit on the main floor rather than confining them to the balcony.

In response to ever-increasing waves of brutality and dehumanization in the twenty-first century, the Department of Justice required that cities and their municipal and federally subsidized law enforcement agencies take responsibility for their history, systems, and cultural constructions that resulted in implicit bias and institutional preservation.[108] Likewise, in our Methodist faith tradition it's time to take responsibility and accept accountability for ourselves and for one another. If our tradition is sincerely striving to align with the word, witness, and will of God, our efforts must live beyond pious ritualistic pageantry and toothless typographic rehearsing of divine imperatives and precepts. Our affirming of

107.   Michael Lipka, "The Most and Least Racially Diverse U.S. Religious Groups," May 30, 2020, https://www.pewresearch.org/fact-tank/2015/07/27/the-most-and-least-racially-diverse-u-s-religious-groups/.

108.   "FAQs on Implicity Bias," US Department of Justice, https://www.jus-tice.gov/opa/file/871121/download.

God's beloved people and their sacred and inalienable worth must materialize in full this time.

Prophetic Witness

Ethical prophetic witness is about telling divine truth—which discloses God's self—by means of unmasking the reality of suffering and leading into the promised hope of God. For example, in 2 Samuel the prophet Nathan is sent by God to David. The prophet makes David look into the mirror to see his infidelity. The prophet's role is to proclaim God's word on behalf of the people as a corrective to systems of power. The prophet reflects upon what they currently are and reminds them of what they ought to be.

Black Methodists and their institutions framed a platform for contesting oppression. It produced leaders, institutions, and resources necessary for African Americans to confront the political, economic, and social infrastructure. Such leaders and institutions remain necessary for redress of contemporary concerns and conditions related to African American and African Diaspora peoples. Hence, when Black folk in Methodism say, "Here I am," we're here to remind "you" how it was . . . is . . . and ought to be.

In this moment, we are called to prophetic responsibilities. First, we have a theocratic responsibility to listen for God's voice amid the noise of our everyday experience and media-drenched culture. In practical terms it is recognizing how and where our faith calls each of us to respond and engage.

Second, we have a democratic responsibility to either invest or reinvest in the individual for collective good. Simply praying for change to come and abstaining from struggling with one to become the change is counterproductive. The "connection" is challenged to genuflect to its own practices, presence (or lack thereof), and perpetuation of race-based inequities. Each of us exists within a net of mutuality, knitted by the thread of our respective sacred personhood. It is a reexamining and aligning of misguided, oppressive, and abusive theological and social constructs toward healthy, loving, and just relationships and practices.

Third, empathic responsibility requires us to engage in faith-filled dialogue and to actively participate ethically in the public square. It embraces a radical love ethic, as well as transformative thought and action. It requires more than good intentions and lip service. It requires us to make ourselves, and maybe those whom we love and respect, feel uncomfortable.

McClain said, "African American Methodists are both a remnant of hope and a reminder of the ideal for their church to match its practice with its proclamation."[109] Despite Black members in Methodism being relegated to a "church-within-a-church," and despite assault on the human dignity of Black lives in our communities, and despite the trials and hardships, the dissolution and decline, our presence is required and essential. No Methodist ministry or lives matter until Black lives matter.

---

109.   McClain, *Black People in the Methodist Church*, 83.

Chapter Ten

I'M BLACK. I'M METHODIST.
I'M CHALLENGING
(TO WHAT END)?

Vance P. Ross

Senior Pastor, Central United Methodist Church, Atlanta, Georgia

I believe that being the church is about pursuing the commonwealth of God, the reign of heaven, for all the people of God. This harmony is the concord envisioned in bountiful living for creation. This harmony is the result of the divine vision for creation, even for the universe.

Conjured up for the express intent of economically abusing Black people and other people of color, the notion of race stands in contradiction to this vision. This false idea infects humanity, perverting Whites to believe that, solely by skin color, they are seen as superior while others are diminished. More specifically, racism gives birth to the ideas infecting White supremacy, and for the exclusive purpose of greed and insistent inferiority for anyone not racialized as White.

Infested with this untruth, Methodism often stands outside of its stated mission. Rather than making disciples of Jesus Christ for the transformation of the world, White supremacy/racism disfigures any ambition the church has toward the God-ordained vision of commonwealth. In so doing, the Black United Methodist Church has found itself in a place of shrinking presence, influence, and witness.

Shall this continue? In a time rife with anxiety over the future, we submit an interesting query: What does it mean to identify as Black and United Methodist? As the pandemic of White supremacy/racism fails to relent—failure not endemic to Methodism alone—shall such identification be foolish and fruitless? Surrounded by this contagion, will The United Methodist Church show appreciation for diversity, rather than contempt?

Black and Methodist: What Is the Priority?

To be Black and Methodist: is it possible? Absolutely. From the inception of Methodism on these shores, William B. McClain makes it clear: an American Methodist Church never existed without Black people. It is a profound truth. Blackness and Methodism do exist in tandem.

While matriculating at the Interdenominational Theological Center (ITC), I entertained the idea of changing denominational affiliation; yet, I saw no essential reason to change. In fact, it was there that I found more reason to remain United Methodist. ITC was and is an ecclesial tapestry. It structured a splendid diversity that encouraged admiration of my own traditions as well as appreciation for the customs of others. The wonder of the varied church traditions there wooed me: Baptist, African Methodist Episcopal, Christian Methodist Episcopal, Church of God in Christ, Presbyterian. This ecumenical mix was steeped in dedication to serve the freedom of God's Black people. I felt beckoned, even called, to enjoy and relish the curiosities and marvels of Black religious diversity. My particular Methodist tradition added to the exquisiteness of the experience.

Now, while United Methodism and Blackness indeed can and should exist together, certain clarifications and distinctions are essential in this regard. On the one hand, my Blackness is my God-given gift. Descending from Africans, from the survivors of a sin-sick and criminal enslavement, honors me in ways I cannot express. The terrorism they overcame for me to be here both repulses and enthuses (en/theo) me. I'm grateful to God for my Blackness.

I'm both agonized and disgusted by the inhumanity of a nation that claimed religious freedom but never defined it as it became . . . a faith in greed, blood-thirst, and immorality. The country announced, even touted, liberty for religious sects. What it demonstrated was freedom for land and labor theft shrouded in religious language and rituals. Entire nations were traumatized so that the United States of America could exist.

By surviving this criminal abuse, my ancestors esteemed me incredibly. That they endured and maintained both joy and love stirs me in overwhelming ways: how to stand for justice and remain in relationship, how to love daily when surrounded by threat, how to keep a mission focus when the racial tempests howl continually. I come from this godly heritage. Contentment and worth saturate me as I consider it. I glory in it. I revel in it. God granted me the privilege, priceless and invaluable, of Blackness. I was born in this.

Following Jesus in the Methodist tradition, on the other hand, is my human choice. This is not something bequeathed by descent. I was not created to this faith or to this denomination.

The divine gift of free will dictated that I could leave it, ignore it, deny it, or even decry it. There is no actual manner in which, truly, I must follow Jesus. This is absolutely true: I didn't have to be Methodist.

See, as a child, most of my playmates and peers were Baptist. Some friends were Church of God in Christ (we called them holiness). Some called themselves Pentecostal. And it seemed to me that their worship experiences were more expressive, their music was more exciting, and their congregations seemed to be more fun. Because of these things, I saw each of these as a possibility for being what I then called a Christian.

But choice enabled me to see some things that were valued in my home. While worship wasn't the most expressive, my Methodist church was the first in my day to open a facility so that young people could dance and have social functions. My Methodist church was hardly alone, but it certainly was a leading church in the state of West Virginia as it struggled with guaranteeing full citizenship rights for Black people. I knew education was a Methodist value and that this denomination did much to train young people as thinkers. I understood Methodists as advocates, as critical actors in the world. These impressed me as a boy.

My grandmother, providentially, assured this. Truelove Jearlyn Ferguson Thompson, my "Mama True," took me to the John Stewart Methodist Church. She escorted me into its worship, its activism. She never discussed it; she baptized me in it. The local National Association for the Advancement of Colored People (NAACP) met to strategize at John Stewart Methodist Church. Pastor C. Anderson Davis served as state NAACP president. The Women's Society of Christian Service—rooted in dignity and equality under God—found me sitting in their local church meetings. I learned Methodism's Works of Piety much later; my grandmother immersed me into its social justice, the Works of Mercy. Steeped in Methodism, I chose such as part of my heritage. I didn't own it, and it didn't own me. It was my adult choice, not a religious inheritance. And in the main, I have not regretted it.

Curiously, my home church, upon desegregation in 1968, took on a White pastor. He was a fine fellow. He believed in Black causes, offered new ministry ideas, and was received admirably by the people of the church. This, the second-largest Black Methodist church in West Virginia, a church pastored—two appointments prior—by a civil rights pastor, was immediately desegregated. Not one of the top-ten White Methodist churches received a Black pastor.

It is out of this experience that I yet believed United Methodism was aspirational, divinely ambitious. This church witnessed to the diversity, to the "multi" world to which I saw commitment and which I experienced. God brings people, all people, together in this gospel. I experienced the viability and possibility of all God's people being together and living justice, living love. I learned that in The Methodist Church and the subsequent United Methodist Church.

As a Black man who chose to be Methodist, this aspiration provoked me to remain with the traditions of my ancestors. They journeyed to and through events and eras, through hatred and biases, to call forth a better church. With Blackness bequeathed as holy, and selecting Methodism because of its promises, they showed faithfulness to the commonwealth of God. Because of their heroism I stayed. But reflection causes fresh interrogation: did the church really want them? Black and Methodist: does the church really want me?

Systemic Results

W. Edwards Deming is thought to have said, "Every system is perfectly designed to get the results it gets."[110] That is to say, when we see the outcomes of any structure or system, we view what they were made to produce. For good or ill, for benefit or harm, what an organization or technique provides is what it is built to deliver. This is a sobering truth, one that needs to be identified and addressed in any organization. This especially speaks to the church: a system is perfectly designed for the results it gets.

Society transformed by religion, world-changing faith, characterized the Methodism I saw on a local level. And this was the history of Methodism. Richard Allen said, "The Methodists were the first people that brought glad tidings to the colored people. I feel thankful I ever heard a Methodist preach."[111] The system produced people who, empowered and emboldened by the spirit, inspired work toward love and justice. Black people gravitated to this message, especially as Methodism opposed the terror of enslavement, the trauma of White supremacy/racism. Methodists demanded no ownership of people, no payment to buy people except to free them. They insisted adherence. No options here. This was obligatory. Black people gladly joined Methodism because Methodism, in divine obedience, avowed the humanity of Black people.

But throughout the nation, Black humanity was obliterated. Financial profits, governmental policies, and the sin of greed joined to create racist attitudes and customs. People racialized as

110. Attributed to Deming but probably altered by Paul Batalden. See the W. Edwards Deming Institute; PO Box 309; Ketchum, ID 83340.

111. Jennifer Woodruff Tait, "'My Chains Fell Off.' Francis Asbury and Richard Allen," *Christian History Magazine*, 114, 21.

White developed processes and structures to repudiate the humanity of Brown and Black people. They especially decided that people racialized as Black would be slaves, creatures of bondage and servitude, whose unpaid labor would enrich the treasure chests of Whites.

The Methodist Church ultimately capitulated. When a Southern bishop inherited enslaved persons, The Methodist Episcopal Church split over the Southern desire to maintain slavery. Meanwhile, the Northern Methodists continued their de facto segregation, the norms of division that caused Richard Allen and Absalom Jones to leave the St. George Church in Philadelphia. The 1939 merger of Methodist communions hinged, in large measure, on assuring a system for segregating Black people from Whites. People worshipped in their own buildings, preached to their own hue, and held denominational responsibility only among their own "people." For good measure, the amalgamated church legislated geographic jurisdictions for Whites. They simultaneously decreed the Central Jurisdiction for Black people, assuring that, in this new Methodism, people stayed with their own "kind," operated out of their own customs, and remained a reflection of the segregated society. In other words, the church mimicked three sinister racial values of the nation: racialized status based on color, separation to preserve power and mores, and finally a patriotic kinship.

This church segregation law derived from the nation's laws. The United States developed Black Codes, Jim Crow and Pig Laws to keep Black people subdued. Subordination and lowliness were tools used specifically to discourage and hinder any notion of equality and humanity. These regulations legally defined Black second-class citizenship, status, and category. The church, refusing to lead by precept or example, proved its own devaluing of humanity by building a set of parallel laws. Rather than showing moral and spiritual leadership, Methodism went along.

Still, at its apex, the Central Jurisdiction found vitality. Clergy and local churches adapted their ministries to accept and overcome the challenge of segregation. While growing and building, the jurisdiction developed ministerial viability despite choosing to remain connected to a church that treated them as lesser. Their clergy were denominationally trained and effective. Their laity knew the church, practiced its faith, and made for important ministry. They sought to both prove their humanity and, nobly, to show the system its sins against them. These persons stayed, aspiring to the hopes of the gospel shown at the beginnings of Methodism.

But what does it mean to prove humanity in the church? When the church holds as sacred Scripture texts birthed in the crucible of oppression, when overcoming the history of exile and occupation is basic to the biblical story, what explanation can there be for ecclesial organizing that subjects an entire people to proving their worth? With oppression as mandated by church policy, these noble Black people embraced the task of meriting humanity. They decided to use the Central Jurisdiction as a means to assist in this quest.

But be clear: the Central Jurisdiction was never meant to assist. Black people decided to make it beneficial. They stayed in a church-mandated jurisdictional structure as second-tier members. The Central Jurisdiction was church promulgated malevolence, a racially driven insult purported as divine decree. Jurisdictions existed and still exist, fundamentally, to separate people and ensure a certain White way of life. Electing clergy and lay church leaders, loyal to the biased and regional practices of particular regions, undergirds this system. Thus, when the Central Jurisdiction ended, the others continued, adding Black people, only and entirely, because policy desegregation was occurring across the nation. (Note: Montgomery, Nashville, Selma, and Birmingham civil rights campaigns all led to desegregating practices prior to the Methodist desegregation.)

So then, what did this 1968 merger mean for The United Methodist Black Church? If the Central Jurisdiction was not meant to assist Black people, what did merger mean? Well, some anecdotal numbers speak to it. Florida has one Black church with two hundred worshippers and has no United Methodist Black presence in Orlando, one of its largest and most populous cities. Los Angeles has one Black church with more than two hundred in worship. Among others, Philadelphia, San Francisco, Newark (NJ), Detroit (proper), Cleveland, and Cincinnati (OH) can all boast that they are not the homes of one United Methodist Black church with two hundred or more in worship.[112] The presence of United Methodist Black laity is not close to what it could or should be for effective witness in the world. The occurrence of United Methodist Black clergy in either large or sparsely populated communities borders on invisibility. There is at least one annual conference, home to a major urban center, which purportedly hasn't ordained a Black man in over ten years. What does this mean for an effective laity witness? How can this be true? A system is designed for the results it gets.

---

112. Statistics are taken from the General Council on Finance and Administration of The United Methodist Church.

What Is the Structural Challenge?

Purportedly designed after the United States arrangement of checks and balances, the United Methodist polity is, in fact, more hierarchical than is openly discussed. The annual conference is documented as the basic body (unit of ministry) of the church. It is the place of clergy membership, fellowship, and appointment; however, annual conferences meet only yearly. Annual meetings curtail generative power and, because of such, lend much less capacity to counteract autocracy. What have annual conference meetings meant for Black churches? What policies and procedures, what programs and opportunities have been sustained to build Black churches, to generate Black clergy?

As a legal body constructed to interpret church discipline, the Judicial Council meets semiannually. It stands in a critical place to countermand both legislative and executive works that stand outside the covenant understandings of the church; however, with more than one hundred annual conferences the world over, it is at least a challenge to address the issues and concerns that may need to come before the court. By sheer numbers, the judiciary cannot offer requisite checks and balances. How has the Judicial Council been able to aid the Black church? Beyond decisions that assist in keeping harm from coming to individual Black people (the case of Bishop Earl Bledsoe as the most stunning and important instance in my memory), how has this entity aided the Black church?

With these questions as to the lack of equalized governance, it stands to reason that the executive/episcopal branch of the church reigns over the church. Yes, it reigns. We can call it governing or administering if we wish. If we like, we can elevate theoretical ideas of checks and balances. They do seem well enough balanced on paper. If we choose, we can speak to representative government, a democracy where the churches and clergy do have vote and voice. Indeed I can say, without hesitation, that I have witnessed much grace and kindness from bishops. I have seen such and have benefited from it. I'm grateful.

I have also seen viciousness. I know of vengeful actions from that office, of denying conference entities to exercise proper powers, appointments, hearings, and opportunities. Programs found extra push, while others were denied or destroyed, solely because a bishop said so. Explanations from laity mattered not. Rationale from clerics made no difference. Ugliness went (and can still go) unchecked and unobstructed, as if these were and are the episcopal prerogative.

Much, if not all this, can happen by virtue of appointment making, the all but unlimited authority to assign and deploy clergy. Bishops can literally decide conference direction, area emphasis, and resource allocation all by the fact of appointive power. In this system, bishops can dictate results because they can appoint clergy. The impact is monumental to laity and local churches. When laity are spiritually guided and empowered on the local level, God uses them to bring spiritual and substantive transformation wherever they are. Such laity exert impact on local communities, districts, and annual conferences. Simply by either ignoring their giftedness or moving their pastors or sometimes both, the executive can significantly impair their Methodist witness.

So it is that by organizational performance of the church—the actual execution of its ministry—the discussion of checks and balances rings hollow. They exist by document. The church is ruled by oligarchy, and the oligarchy stands because of:

1. the aforementioned limits on checks and balances;

2. the mandated, elected position of "bishop for life"; or

3. a clergy system that can be traced through the Anglican and Roman Catholic churches into the Caesar-led structure of the Roman Empire.

The executive branch of the church, led by the episcopacy and often through varied allied agencies, functions with an enormous amount of almost unbridled, vested, and consigned power.

Before this critique is dismissed as an attack on the system I spent the previous thirty-five years in, understand that attack is not my quest. Instead, I'm inviting The United Methodist Church, through which I have given my life as a follower of Jesus, to acknowledge and confess what its structures mean and have meant for the Black church. Repentance can only come from that which is recognized and admitted. For Black people, this church has not been the benevolent presence it often seeks to declare. I offer this not so much as an indictment as a disclosure, more a revealing than a condemnation. The results remain sure. They can hardly be ignored. Many, if not most, of the following actions employed by The UMC are to the detriment of its witness among United Methodists. Hardly exhaustive, among the results are these:

1. stripping Black clergy talent from Black local churches by offering higher salaries in connectional positions beyond the local church;

2. contributing to the vanishing presence of Methodists in predominantly Black populated cities and towns;

3. reducing available clergy to serve in local churches;

4. assigning apportionments to churches at the same percentages when every index shows Black income and wealth significantly less than that of Whites;

5. selling properties of White churches to Black churches that become nightmarish to sustain;

6. selling Black-built properties after their closing with proceeds placed in annual conference coffers, never attending to how those proceeds might be used for ministry among those whose people built the Black churches;

7. decrying, demeaning, or ending Black church assistance programs because they were declared "ineffective" by entities who created problems at the program's inception;

8. rendering invisible or silencing Black people when elected as directors to general church boards and agencies;

9. failing to relate the gospel to the situations of young, Black people, causing Black youth and young adults to become "refugees" to other denominations and churches;

10. making token clergy appointments or laity assignments where Black people are to be seen, not heard;

11. forcing early retirements for clergy who have been told there is "no place" for them in the appointive process.

Much of this was predicted at the completed merger in 1972. Black Methodists for Church Renewal, upon its inception, predicted and challenged the church not to move in these ways. Many things could have been shifted, altered, changed or put aside. They were not.

Instead, the denomination clung assiduously to systemic patriotism, a dedication to the structures and processes of United Methodism as conceived. Following the process became a mantra, following without inspection, without consideration of the impact to the Black church. As such, the system's consequences for the Black church have been barely noted, much less examined or critiqued. The results have been unfavorable at best; unkind at worst.

What Are We Going to Do Now?

To be sure, this is no call for the abolition of United Methodism. I'm one who is not in favor of schism, of divorce. I know, from personal experience, the anguish and hurt of splitting. While it can be necessary, there is never anything easy in it. Even in abusive relationships, leaving can be almost impossible.

For Black people, this relationship has been offensive at best, unhealthy at worst. Whatever the intent, the results make the detrimental impact abundantly clear. This is because there has never been a clear call to systemic change that would be in the best interests of the Black church. There has never been a movement that sought to change the effects on the Black church by making the needed systemic changes. Rather than just leave, immediately, there can indeed be change in results. In order to do that, there must be change in the system.

A change in results requires an admission that the present outcomes do not meet missional needs; that is to say, we ought not expect changed outcomes while employing the same system. It cannot be overstated: A system is perfectly designed for the results it gets. United Methodist Black church results, in the main, have not been good. Its population has been overlooked. Its gifts to the church have been manipulated.

What shall we do? First, we must decide to extinguish the lie of race by challenging the sin of White supremacy/racism. Difference is not a synonym for deficient. Living into God's vision requires that the church eliminate this stain on its soul. Second, we must be honest that this system gets what it is designed for: a denomination that structurally reduces Black presence. This can be reversed but only intentional systemic changes will reverse this decline. Third, and foremost, we must clarify our position regarding the mission of the church. Is our mission really to make disciples of Jesus Christ? White supremacy has stifled the witness far too long; that happens because the church has been formed that way. A system is perfectly designed for the results it gets. To enjoy the precious reality of God's diversity, we must alter our system, realizing no structure can be more sacrosanct than the mission of the church and the reign of God.

No reason exists to believe that White supremacy/racism will soon be removed from society. Its inexorable presence and wicked potency feel never-ending. This disease is here to stay, impairing both the church and the nation in death-dealing ways. Still, the faith we claim declares it can be overcome. It can at least be quarantined—rendered impotent—if not totally eradicated by the power of the Holy Spirit and the diligence of the church.

So then, what does it mean to identify as Black and United Methodist? Is such identification ridiculous and futile? It has not been nor does it have to be now. The results do make it clear: for such identification to have significance to the mission, the system needs to change.

CPSIA information can be obtained
at www.ICGtesting.com
Printed in the USA
LVHW040530150121
676514LV00006B/7

9 781791 017095